A Strength-Based Approach to Career Development Using Appreciative Inquiry

Donald A. Schutt, Jr., Ph.D.
University of Wisconsin-Madison

National Career Development Association

A founding division of the American Counseling Association

© Copyright 2007 by the National Career Development Association
   305 North Beech Circle
   Broken Arrow, OK 74012
   Phone: (866) 367-6232
   Fax: (918) 663-7058

Library of Congress Cataloging-in-Publication Data

Schutt, Donald A.
  A Strength-based approach to career development using appreciative inquiry / by Don Schutt
    p. cm.

ISBN 978-1-885333-18-6 (alk. paper)
1. Career development.   I. Title.

HF5381.S424 2007
650. 14--cd22

2007023484

Contents

Preface

This monograph introduces a new approach to career development — one which applies the systems approach of Appreciative Inquiry to the process of finding one's life passion. It is a "Strength-Based Approach" to career development using the process of Appreciative inquiry that focuses on building upon strengths rather than on fixing or repairing deficits. It suggests that the questions we ask drive the direction and focus of our actions and behaviors. The Strength-Based Approach to career development is based on the simple assumptions that every individual has something that works well and that these strengths can be the starting point for creating positive change.

This approach focuses on discovering the best in people and in the relevant world around them. It is the art and practice of asking unconditionally positive questions that strengthen an individual's capacity to comprehend, anticipate, and heighten positive potential. Instead of negation, criticism, and a spiraling diagnosis, there is discovery, dream, design, and destiny. In short, it is an approach that builds on strengths and manages around weaknesses.

The purpose of this process is to create a positive self-image along with the ability to envision even greater possibilities for the future based on individual strengths. The process connects work and life decisions to life partners and support networks. The end result is a better understanding of the "life-giving" forces that provide vitality and distinctive competence to life and work.

The primary technique used in this approach is an appreciative interview, from which the rest of the process unfolds. The appreciative interview uses stories to uncover information or data. It is a process that attempts to discover the best of "what is" for the individual.

The Strength-Based Approach to career development is not a new tool, nor is it a new theory of career development; it is an approach that can be integrated into many different theoretical perspectives.

As a career development professional, using the Strength-Based Approach to career development is refreshing — participants are eager, excited, and motivated to take action. The reframing of career development interventions using the Strength-Based Approach offers individuals an energizing way to assess, explore, and plan for a more positive work-life balance. If the goal is to create an action plan that honors an individual's strengths and articulates her or his hopes for the future, the Strength-Based Approach provides a process for reaching that goal.

The development of this monograph came about as a result of a number of key people who nurtured, supported, and guided me through this project. I have greatly appreciated the support from NCDA, most notably Mary Ann Powell for her project management and thoughtful communication. I want to thank Judy Ettinger for keeping me on task, reading and editing the drafts, and talking me through the process. Her impact and influence over the years has been important to my professional development and I greatly value her as a colleague.

I have also been fortunate to have had many mentors in my career journey. David Jepsen took a risk many years ago when he invited me to teach a career development class to undergraduate students at the University of Iowa. Teaching that class and working with him changed the direction of my career. I would also like to acknowledge Roger Lambert who offered me an opportunity to work at the Center on Education and Work at the University of Wisconsin-Madison. It was one of the best learning experiences I could have ever imagined, and Roger's perspective, entrepreneurial spirit, and thoughtful nature are forever embedded in my work.

The final thanks go to my family. I am the luckiest person in the world to have a partner who supports and nurtures my work, and two sons who understand my passions.

I. Shifting to a Strength-Based Approach

This chapter introduces the idea of using Appreciative Inquiry (AI) in the career development process. The concept of modifying traditional career development questions of "who am I?," "where am I going?," and "how do I get there?" is transformed to "discovery, dream, design, and destiny," also called the "4-D Cycle."

Career Development and Appreciative Inquiry

As a career development professional, you have likely been trained to help your clients, students, or participants to identify their values, skills, and abilities related to the world of work, to generate options about how they could fit into the world of work, and to strategize about how to achieve their goals. This process is the foundation of the field and has been practiced successfully over time. A competent professional will always ask, "Is there a way to enhance these time-tested practices?"

What if career development discussions focused on looking at the client's, student's, or participant's experiences when things were going well, in situations when they felt most excited and successful? What if every question you asked was seen as both a prompt for gathering information and also as a strategy for influencing behavior?

This monograph introduces a new approach to career development – one which applies the systems approach of Appreciative Inquiry to the process of finding one's life passion. It is a "Strength-Based Approach" to career development using the process of Appreciative Inquiry. In this chapter, interventions are approached from the perspective of the career development professional guiding an individual through the "Building on your Strengths" process. This chapter provides an overview, foundational concepts, important definitions, comparisons to other approaches, and caveats. Chapter II offers an abbreviated history of and background on Appreciative Inquiry. A more detailed analysis and discussion of the Strength-Based Approach is the focus of Chapter III. Chapter IV demonstrates one application of this approach through a workshop setting.

Appreciative Inquiry is typically applied to systems rather than individuals. Since Appreciative Inquiry is a systems approach and the Strength-Based Approach is focused on individual career development, this monograph adapts the system approach to the individual. The groundwork leading up to that adaptation begins at the system level with Appreciative Inquiry. Appreciative Inquiry "is a collaborative and highly participative, system-wide approach to seeking, identifying, and enhancing the 'life-giving forces' that are present when a system is performing optimally in human, economic, and organizational terms" (Watkins & Mohr, 2001, p. 14). Watkins and Mohr (2001) also provided this summary of Appreciative Inquiry:

> Appreciative Inquiry is an approach to the development of human systems that recognizes that we can choose the view that either (1) Human systems are primarily constellations of problems/obstacles to be analyzed and overcome, or (2) Human systems contain mysterious life-giving forces to be understood and embraced.
>
> Appreciative Inquiry recognizes that whichever assumption we make about the nature of reality, the choice will lead us to a certain focus in our conversations. And those conversations will in turn lead to action at both the conscious and unconscious levels.
>
> Appreciative Inquiry uses the power of inquiry to engage our imagination, which in turn influences our actions. By focusing through inquiry on that which is life-giving, that which is energizing, that which is joyful and fun, and by amplifying those qualities by involving the "whole system" in co-construction and co-innovation based on the finding of the inquiry, AI enables systems to transform themselves. (p. 61)

The translation to individual terms is an easy one — seeking, identifying, and enhancing the life-giving forces when achieving an optimal balance over the course of the lifespan. The Strength-Based Approach to career development is the realization of the life-giving forces in creating a work-life balance.

The extension of the Strength-Based Approach to individual career development, and, more specifically, to the work-life balance component, is viewed in the terms laid out in Hansen's (1997) Integrative Life Planning model (defined later in this chapter) which encourages a systemic view of the individual when considering work and life decisions, and engages the connections between self, community, and the greater society. An example that might demonstrate this approach comes out of the story of the educational consultant who decided to change jobs. The consultant had what he described as the "best job of his life." It drew on his creativity, his writing and presenting skills, his teaching skills, and his passion for education and, specifically, his interest in career development. The job offered him opportunities to write, work on software development, and engage other professionals across the country in developing more effective educational systems. The challenge for this consultant was that he was beginning to spend more time traveling and working out of state than he was at home with his young family. He realized that while he had the best job of his life, he had an undesirable life. Somewhere along his career progression, his focus became narrowed toward his work, away from the other important people and things in his life; his sense of work-life balance was skewed toward work. For one of the first times in his life, he engaged his immediate family in the discussion about his career.

Together, they identified the components of his work that gave him the most satisfaction — the teaching, the ability to be creative, the entrepreneurial prospects, and most importantly the opportunities for creating an impact on others through education. He and his partner also considered their life system — their infant son, other family members in the community, and the type of life they envisioned. After identifying those important and positive, energizing characteristics, he began to look for a new job.

The result was that he was able to find another job that required much less travel, was nearly as enjoyable as his previous job (and that also built on his strengths and passion), and one that offered him the opportunity to spend time at home with his family. This story exemplifies an appreciative approach to career development and illustrates using the combination of life-giving forces to find a better work-life balance.

In many ways, the "Building on your Strengths" approach is an individual's articulated narrative relative to personal strengths, passions, and successes. It is about looking at those times when things are going well, developing an image of what one wants, learning from others how they have been successful, and creating an image that can be continually regenerated and that is then used as a guide for one to plan the future. At the simplest level, one outcome is achieving satisfaction and success by building on personal strengths and managing around weaknesses.

Moving Toward a Strength-Based Approach

The Strength-Based Approach is just that, an approach. It is both a way of thinking and a way of behaving that is broad and at the foundation of the work being done. In this way, the Strength-Based Approach, much like Appreciative Inquiry, is not intended to be seen as a tool or a strategy used for a narrowly focused intervention. This approach requires the ability to change our focus from problem-solving and deficit-based (or "find-the-fixes" approach) to a process of seeking what has been successful and going well, and asking how we could do more of those things. It is a change in the way we see the world and the application of that view to career development.

One example from the workplace is drawn from the system that people use for evaluating performance. Performance reviews often center on getting both positive feedback as well as defining areas for improvement. After one leaves the review session, how often does one focus on "areas for improvement" versus the positive information? If in that meeting, 5 minutes were spent on improvements and 55 minutes on the areas where one exceeded expectations, what would be remembered the most? Following the meeting, does one focus on the 5 minutes or the 55 minutes? The point is that feedback from educational experiences, from the workplace, and from society influences the picture one has of oneself which, in turn, potentially creates from all the multiple possible realities a reality that improvement is needed rather than a feeling of success and satisfaction. The resulting shift in focus creates an "overcoming deficiencies" approach rather than a "building on strengths" approach. The connection between the focus chosen (strength-based versus deficit-based) and self-concept and, in a more specific sense, occupational self-concept, highlights the importance of considering the Strength-Based Approach.

The significance of this connection from a career development perspective is great. Super, Savickas, and Super (1996) wrote, "[a] career can be viewed as the life course of a person encountering a series of developmental tasks and attempting to handle them in such a way as to become the kind of person he or she wants to be" (p. 140). If the outcome of those developmental tasks is not framed effectively, the impact is both immediate (self-confidence) and long-lasting, as suggested in this earlier excerpt from the same chapter:

Career self-concept theory concentrates on the

personal meaning of abilities, interests, values, and choices as well as how they coalesce into life themes. This subjective perspective helps clients to understand facts and experience in their own terms. Purpose, not traits, is the emphasis of the subjective approach to conceptualizing the self.

Objective measures identify a person's similarity to others, whereas subjective assessment reveals the person's uniqueness. Consider interest assessment as an example. Objective measures of interests identify the strength of an interest relative to some comparison group, whereas subjective stories reveal the origins of the interest in a life history, the contemporary expression of the interest, and the possible future use of that interest in pursuing goals and values. (p. 139)

Approaching career development from a strength-based approach reinforces an occupational self-concept that captures the positive life themes for use in setting future life and career goals.

Foundational Concepts

There was a shelter in Iowa that provided a safe haven for women and children who were battered, emotionally abused, or in otherwise difficult situations. The women were often faced with making very tough decisions about their own life as well as the lives of their children. It took a great deal of courage for them to make the choice to leave their current situations for unsure futures. When the women entered the shelter, as part of meeting their physical and emotional needs, the emphasis was not on the horrible things that had brought these women to the safe house, but rather on the power it took for them to make a tough decision and risk seeking a new life. The focus was on each individual as a survivor rather than a victim. It was amazing to see the impact of this centering on strengths as the women began to make new lives and carry forward the best of who they were. While this emphasis was not described as a strength-based approach, at its core it captures the concepts.

Although the next chapter covers Appreciative Inquiry (AI) in greater detail, there are some foundational concepts which are useful to discuss here. In Appreciative Inquiry, there is an assumption that all systems have untapped, rich stories which can be accessed through interviews, dialogue with others, guided imagery, and through the identification of themes, patterns, and life-giving forces. Interviews also connect with the notion that through conversation

we create new images that lead to new actions and behaviors. Hammond (1996) identified eight assumptions of Appreciative Inquiry:

1. In every society, organization, or group, something works.
2. What we focus on becomes our reality.
3. Reality is created in the moment, and there are multiple realities.
4. The act of asking questions of an organization or group influences the group in some way.
5. People have more confidence and comfort to journey into the future (the unknown) when they carry forward parts of the past (the known).
6. If we carry parts of the past forward, they should be what is best about the past.
7. It is important to value differences.
8. The language we use creates our reality. (pp. 20–21)

Revisiting the example presented earlier in this section depicts an Appreciative Inquiry or Strength-Based Approach applied on an individual level. In working with the women entering the shelter, the focus was on what worked for them. By doing so, it focused on the strengths the women had that they could then take more confidently into the future.

The Appreciative Inquiry process varies depending on the context of the inquiry and is guided by the "four Ds": discovery, dream, design, and destiny (Cooperrider & Whitney, 2005). Cooperrider, Whitney, and Stavros (2005) describe the systems approach of Appreciative Inquiry as "a form of organizational study that selectively seeks to locate, highlight, and illuminate what are referred to as the 'life-giving' forces of the organization's existence, its positive core" (p. 4). In the initial phase of an Appreciative Inquiry, two questions are behind any undertaking:

1. What, in this particular setting and context, gives life to this system — when is it most alive, healthy, and symbiotically related to its various communities?
2. What are the possibilities, expressed and latent, that provide opportunities for more effective (value-congruent) forms of organizing?
(Cooperrider, Whitney, & Stavros, 2005, p. 4)

Also critical to the process is the appreciative interview. "The uniqueness and power of an AI interview

8

stem from its fundamentally affirmative focus. What distinguishes AI at this phase is that every question is positive" (Cooperrider & Whitney, 2005, pp. 25-26).

Appreciative Inquiry is intended to be used as an organizational approach to evaluate systems, but these questions and the positive framing have great relevance to individuals, as is demonstrated in Chapters III and IV.

The interview and the ensuing dialogue in this search for strengths and life-giving forces provide the career development professional with an opportunity to help the individual develop her or his thoughts in a focused way. It also provides an opportunity to hear what comes through to others in her or his words. In short, Appreciative Inquiry is a strategy for intentional change because it identifies the best of "what is" and "what could be," a process for engaging people in an effort to choose consciously to seek out inquiry into that which is generative and life enriching; and it is a way of seeing the world that is attentive to and affirming of one's best and highest qualities.

At the foundation of this Strength-Based Approach to career development are five critical concepts:

1. Each individual has rich, untapped stories that, when accessed through a positively-framed appreciative interview, provide glimpses into important patterns, themes, and life-giving forces.
2. As these surface, self-understanding relative to successes, strengths, passions, energy, and resources comes into greater focus as do the circumstances and people who play supporting roles.
3. With that understanding and focus, one is able to make decisions about which of those positive components to carry forward in planning a future work-life scenario.
4. The future work-life scenario is strengthened by an expanded sense of the conditions, contexts, and people that facilitate drawing on the best and highest qualities.
5. The language used will continue to focus energy in positive ways, helping to choose a reality that draws on strengths and articulates a hopeful future.

Also important to these concepts is an understanding of the underlying definitions supporting this approach.

Important Guiding Definitions

The following definitions are included to clarify the terms that are used throughout this monograph. They are inserted at this point to enhance the descriptions that follow. The next chapter also provides a more detailed description of Appreciative Inquiry.

Appreciative Inquiry (AI)

Appreciative Inquiry is an approach to seeing the world, as well as a process. It "is about the co-evolutionary search for the best in people, their organizations, and the relevant world around them. In its broadest focus, it involves systematic discovery of what gives 'life' to a living system when it is most alive, most effective, and most constructively capable in economic, ecological, and human terms. AI involves, in a central way, the art and practice of asking questions that strengthen a system's capacity to apprehend, anticipate, and heighten positive potential" (Cooperrider & Whitney, 2000, p. 5).

Career

Defined as the "totality of work — paid and unpaid — one does in a lifetime" (National Career Development Association Web site, http://www.ncda.org/pdf/Policy.pdf).

Career Development

"The total constellation of psychological, sociological, educational, physical, economic, and chance factors that combine to influence the nature and significance of work in the total lifespan of any given individual" (National Career Development Association Web site, http://www.ncda.org/pdf/Policy.pdf).

Integrative Life Planning (Hansen, 1997)

A comprehensive career development model, Integrative Life Planning, that brings together many aspects of people's lives in ways that help them to see the "big picture" of their lives, their communities, and the larger society. It is both a philosophical framework and a set of practical strategies that work in harmony with concepts like connectedness, pluralism, spirituality, subjectivity, wholeness and community. It embraces the notions of patterns as fluid, integrative processes that bring parts together to make a whole and the need for reflection on one's developmental priorities for mind, body, and spirit.

There are six important principles to Integrative Life Planning: It is a way of seeing the world that takes into account both personal development and the contexts within which we live by focusing on the values of diversity and inclusivity; examining the relationship goals and achievement goals relative to society, the organization, the family, and the individual; exploring connections and links between work and family; introducing spirituality, meaning, and purpose as key aspects of life planning; and helping people manage change and understand their life choices, decisions, and transitions in a societal context (adapted from Hansen, 1997, pp. 11–18).

Life-giving Forces

Those distinctive strengths that give life and vitality when functioning at your best are life-giving forces (adapted from Watkins & Mohr, 2001, p. 75). These could include elements or experiences within the past and/or present that represent individual strengths when operating at the very best and could be a single moment in time or any aspect that contributes to the highest points and most valued experiences or characteristics (modified from Cooperrider, Whitney, & Stavros, 2005).

Positive Core

Cooperrider and Whitney (2005) describe the positive core of Appreciative Inquiry as "one of the greatest and largely unrecognized resources in the field of change management today" (p. 8). It is derived from the assumption that "every organization and community have many untapped and rich accounts of the positive — what people talk about as past, present, and future capacities, or the positive core" (Cooperrider & Whitney, 2005, p. 8). Through experience and in the context of Appreciative Inquiry, Cooperrider and Whitney (2005) articulated the definition of "positive core" in this:

> Human systems grow in the direction of what they persistently ask questions about, and this propensity is strongest and most sustainable when the means and ends of the inquiry are positively correlated. The single most important action a group can take to liberate the human spirit and consciously construct a better future is to make the positive core the common and explicit property of all. (p. 9)

Positive Possibilities

Also referred to as "provocative propositions," positive possibilities are statements that bridge the best of "what is" with a vision of "what might be." As such, it becomes a written expression of the desired state, written in the present tense, to guide planning and success in the future (modified from Cooperrider, Whitney & Stavros, 2005, p. 419).

Blending Career Development and Appreciative Inquiry

The blending of career development and Appreciative Inquiry is best articulated by comparing a traditional career development approach (on the individual level) to an organizational systems approach influenced by the Appreciative Inquiry. The goal is to assist an individual in building a plan based on the personal components that are strengths and passions rather than a plan that is centered on working around the barriers. In other words, how do you help individuals create a plan that capitalizes on strengths and manages around weaknesses? This will be considered from career and Appreciative Inquiry perspectives ending in a blended approach.

Traditional Approach to Career Development

This approach is based on the belief that career development emerges from a lifelong dynamic interaction between the individual and environment. As such, that dynamic interaction progresses through a process of self-understanding, an understanding of the world of work, and consequently finding the personal connection to the world of work that leads to satisfying and successful lifelong engagement in both paid and unpaid experiences.

One model for looking at that process involves three dimensions — "who am I?", "where am I going?", and "how do I get there?" — through which individuals move over time. The progression in this model is from assessment to exploration to action.

The first dimension, as seen in Figure 1, raises the question "who am I?" This area is where people typically begin. In schools, the result of testing usually leads to a discussion of aptitudes and skills. Next, depending on the outcome of the assessment, decisions are made as a part of the process of planning for the future. For example, a student is assessed in 8th grade, and the results of the assessment are used to help the student develop her or his high school course schedule. The course schedule typically prepares the student to either go on to higher education or to go to work. The extent to which the 8th-grade student (and parents) is involved depends on the teachers and the counselors. The student enters high school, completes the courses, and goes on to the next career step (college or work).

Figure 1. Who Am I?

Assessment

Who Am I?
- Life Priorities
- Interests
- Preferences
- Aptitudes

and discuss the requirements, daily tasks, and rewards of their work. The student hears the information and then might set goals.

The third dimension, shown in Figure 3, "How Do I Get There?," is seen as the action area. This area might include attending workshops on interviewing or networking and career problem solving when challenges arise. It is also the area where decisions about post–high school training and higher education are discussed. Years ago, the process ended at the action area because employers would typically tailor their employee development programs around "who am I?" The issues of "where am I going?" were also handled by the employer in terms of career ladders within the organization or promotion decisions. More and more today, this process of assessment, exploration, and action has become more cyclical and ongoing, and is often in the hands of individuals rather than the employer.

Figure 3. How Do I Get There?

Figure 2. Where Am I Going?

Exploration

Where Am I Going?
- Career Information
- Labor Market Inforomation
- Career Research
- Goal Setting

Action

How Do I Get There?
- Skills to Develop
- Education / Training
- Self-Marketing Activities
- Obstacles / Strategies

The next dimension in the process is depicted in Figure 2, "Where Am I Going?" It focuses on the acquisition of career- and workforce-related information and the integration of that data with goal setting. Prior to the explosion of the Internet, getting this information was challenging. Now, the information is so readily available that the challenge is knowing how to use the information and discerning useful information from the rest. An example in this area might be a career day in a high school where workers in different fields come

This approach reflects a more traditional model. When combined together as shown in Figure 4, it also characterizes the process that many people go through to determine their future work life. The process of responding to the three questions has also served as an organizing structure for career centers, career-development product developers, and career-development delivery systems. The Strength-Based Approach to career development utilizes the traditional career development process as a foundational framework with which Appreciative Inquiry is blended.

Figure 4. Career Development Process

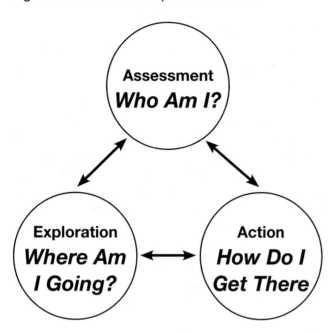

An Appreciative Inquiry Approach

Watkins & Mohr (2001) identified five core processes that are depicted in Figure 5, "Key Appreciative Inquiry Processes." Since the language originally was focused on a systems approach, Figure 5 expresses the concepts in terms that are more broad and suited to a focus on individuals so as to fit with the Strength-Based Approach (there has been a slight modification from the original source). The first process centers on choosing a positive focus. This requires choosing to focus energy on identifying the times when things are going well, and avoiding the often natural habit of spotlighting challenges, problems, and tougher times. This process is about identifying and trying to replicate that which is powerful, positive, and potent for the individual. This connects back to the example provided earlier in which we focus our attention on positive or negative feedback following a performance review. It means career development professionals need to work with individuals to move from a problem-solving mode to increasing the focus on understanding individual strengths and passions.

The second process, inquiring into life-giving forces, is the point at which the career development professional engages in an Appreciative Inquiry interview with the individual to explore the patterns, themes, and life-giving forces that emerge. This interview also elicits information used in an analysis of themes in the third process as topics are selected for further explo-

ration. In the approach discussed in this monograph, there is also an opportunity to expand on the examination of themes by using an imagery activity.

Figure 5. Key Appreciative Inquiry Processes

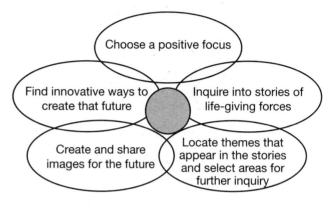

Adapted from Watkins & Mohr, 2001, p. 40.

Once the themes and life-giving forces have been identified, an image for the preferred future (the fourth process) is created. This draws on the more visual stimuli of the imagery which is then continually regenerated as a support and reminder of the picture of the ideal work-life scenario. This naturally leads into the fifth process of finding ways to create that future. These processes are important as they lay the foundation for the Appreciative Inquiry processes.

Watkins and Mohr (2001) stated that "Appreciative Inquiry's potential comes from the integration of (1) *a practical change process* and (2) *a new paradigm of how we shape our future*" (p. 24). This practical change process is best described by using the 4-D Cycle which is a model that describes the four phases of an Appreciative Inquiry (see Figure 6.). According to Cooperrider, Whitney, & Stavros (2005), the assumption is that there "is a 'solution to be embraced,' rather than a 'problem to be solved'" (p. 5). They continued by describing the cycle in the following way:

> It starts with selecting a topic: affirmative topic choice. What follows are *Discovery* (appreciating and valuing), *Dream* (envisioning), *Design* (co-constructing the future), and *Destiny* (learning, empowering, and improvising to sustain the future). These are the essence of dialogue woven through each step of the process. (p.5)

Figure 6. The Phases of the 4-D Cycle

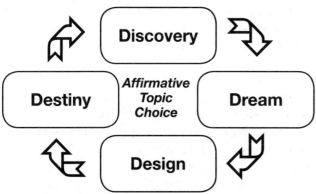

Adapted from Cooperrider, Whitney, & Stavros, 2005, p. 30.

The phases of Appreciative Inquiry demonstrate the systems approach to finding the "best of what is" and implementing a process to build "the best" into future organizational structures. The next section blends the traditional career development process with Appreciative Inquiry to create the Strength-Based Approach.

The Strength-Based Blended Approach

Overlaying the 4-D Cycle onto the three questions model ("who am I?," "where am I going?," and "how do I get there?") of the career development process creates the framework for the Strength-Based Approach to career development. This works conceptually as both the career development process and the Appreciative Inquiry approach as depicted in the 4-D Cycle each represent a progression through which data are discovered, analyzed, and used for creating action through planning. In the case of career development, the focus is on the individual; in the case of Appreciative Inquiry, the focus is on all the systems in an organization. The Strength-Based Approach embodies the focus on the individual with the positive approach of Appreciative Inquiry to redefine the career development process.

There are a number of assumptions that are necessary for this intersection to be useful.

1. Both individuals and organizations change and grow over time. Sometimes that change relates to identity, sometimes to purpose, and sometimes that change is in response to continuous shifts in the environment. It is helpful to have processes in place to work with the change.

2. Within each person and organization, there are rich, untapped stories that provide insights into what is important. Those insights are transparent as well as hidden below the surface.

3. There are certain conditions under which both individuals and organizations flourish. It is possible to identify what those conditions are and how to create and sustain those conditions.

4. Where organizations and individuals focus their time, energy, and resources is the direction in which they will tend to head. A change in perspective, for example focusing on the best of what is that gives energy and excitement, might provide an alternative equal (or better) endpoint.

5. Career development and Appreciative Inquiry are complex; therefore, it is important to have a strong sense of the competencies and skills necessary to be successful in the approach chosen.

6. Individuals and organizations do not exist (typically) in isolation, but rather they are engaged at nearly every moment in economic, environmental, and human systems.

These assumptions are important in that career development and Appreciative Inquiry share common ground that allows the application of the system tool (which is what Appreciative Inquiry is intended to be) to a typically individual process such as career development.

How does this happen? To move to a "strength-based" approach, each of the three circles represented by the questions "who am I?," "where am I going?," and "how do I get there?" is linked to the phases described in Appreciative Inquiry's 4-D Cycle. The career development process and the Appreciative Inquiry approach integrate into a single system (Figure 7, The Strength-Based Approach). In Figure 7, the circles still represent the career development processes and the descriptors within each circle embody an Appreciative Inquiry approach (see Appendix A for a more detailed view). The Strength-Based Approach to career development provides a detailed graphic of the process including the critical questions and focus of each phase of the process.

The "who am I?" question in the career development process transitions to the "discovery" phase from Appreciative Inquiry where the critical question becomes "what gives life?" This transition retains the career development influence of self-understanding and the focus becomes cast in a positive perspective as "appreciating."

The "where am I going?" question transitions to the "dream" phase, with exploration still the critical task and envisioning the positive framing. Critical questions to be addressed are "what might be?" and "what is the world calling for?"

Figure 7. The Strength-Based Approach

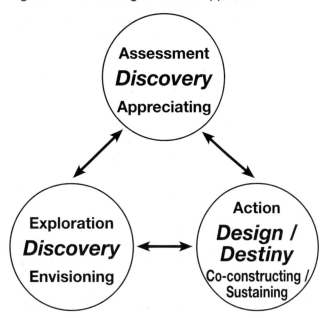

The "where am I going?" question is still action oriented and now captures both the "design" and "destiny" phases. The shift created by applying Appreciative Inquiry modifies the tasks as co-constructing (connected to the design phase) and sustaining (connected to the destiny phase). In the design phase, the critical question is "what should be the ideal?" "How to empower, learn, and adjust/improvise?" is the important question in the destiny phase.

The blending of career development and Appreciative Inquiry and the integration of the developmental processes sets the stage for a Strength-Based Approach to career development using Appreciative Inquiry.

A Strength-Based Approach to Career Development

The goal of the Strength-Based Approach to career development is to create an action plan that honors a person's strengths and articulates her or his hopes for the future. The keys to this process are (a) finding the seeds of excellence on which to develop, (b) creating images of excellence in hopes that the individual moves toward those images, and (c) developing a plan that engages all the important people and forces in a person's life.

The Process

The purpose of this process is to create a positive self-image and allow the individual to envision even greater possibilities based on strengths. The process also connects work and life decisions to others who serve as life partners and support networks. Chapter III details how this process is engaged; supporting activities can be found in Appendix B.

The process can be used in a group setting such as a workshop (as will be demonstrated in Chapter III) or by career development professionals working with individuals or small groups. This is a brief outline of the process:

I. Introduction to the Process
II. Discovery Phase
   a. The Appreciative Interview
   b. Images of My Positive Future
III. Dream Phase
   a. Locating My Personal Themes
   b. My Ideal Work-Life Scenario
IV. Design Phase
   a. Innovative Ways to Create My Future: My Sequence for Success
   b. Sequence for Success: Shoulds, Wants, & Will
   c. Action Plan: My "WILL DO" Goal
   d. Cultivating My Sequence for Success
V. Destiny Phase
   a. Possible Bumps in the Road to Building on My Strengths
   b. Sustaining My Positive Possibilities
VI. Valuing the Process of Building on My Strengths

The process detailed here is one of many ways that Appreciative Inquiry can be applied to career development. Each intervention can and should vary according to the needs of the individual and the situation.

The application of this process to a classroom setting will be discussed in greater detail in Chapter III including a more detailed description of the activities.

A Comparative Look at Other Strength-Focused Approaches

How does this approach compare to developmental assets or other strength-focused materials? Several studies have identified similar processes on which programs have been created. For this discussion, four such structures will be identified: the work on developmental assets by the Search Institute, the Gallup data reported by Buckingham and Coffman (1999) and later expanded to the individual level by Buckingham and Clifton (2001), and the "Signature Strengths" approach by Peterson and Seligman (2004) which leads to the positive psychology movement.

Developmental Assets

The Search Institute, a non-profit research group based in Minneapolis, Minnesota has been researching the success of young people since the late 1950s. Their research has identified 40 developmental assets important to young people. Benson (2003) described developmental assets as ". . . represent[ing] a theoretical construct identifying a set of environmental and intrapersonal strengths known to enhance educational and health outcomes for children and adolescents" (p. 19). He continued, "The 40 elements in this framework represent a synthesis of multiple research literatures and are purposefully positioned as health-enhancing resources over which communities have considerable control" (p. 19). The Search Institute (2007) described the process: "asset building really isn't about perfection. It's about facilitating and helping to nurture the opportunities, skills, relationships, values, and self-perceptions that all young people need and deserve. That foundation of strengths will then help them navigate and thrive in a world that certainly isn't perfect."

The 40 assets are divided into four categories of external assets and four categories of internal assets. The external asset categories are support, empowerment, boundaries and expectations, and constructive use of time. The internal assets are commitment to learning, positive values, social competencies, and positive identity (Benson, 2003).

The Search Institute's developmental assets provide a structure within which schools and communities can share a common language with parents and others concerned about the growth and development of young people today. These assets differ in form and in purpose with the Strength-Based Approach taken in this monograph. The key distinguishing differences are:

- The Search Institute has identified 40 specific assets where the Strength-Based Approach has an undefined and nearly unlimited number of assets.
- The assets are defined by the client or participants in the Strength-Based Approach.
- The purpose of the developmental assets program is for community-based engagement on issues related to schools and young people in

contrast to the Strength-Based Approach's focus on individual development within the family and other support systems.
- The basis for the information comes from data and research studies for the developmental assets compared to the data coming from individual life experiences in the Strength-Based Approach.

The common ground is creating a positive future.

Gallup Data

Buckingham and Coffman (1999) used 25 years of survey data of more than one million employees, combined with a more specific meta-analysis of data from a 1998 Gallup survey of more than 105,000 employees from more than 2,500 business units, to identify what the best managers do. This data, combined with in-depth interviews with more than 80,000 managers in 400 companies, helped them to identify 12 questions that lead to better understanding of what the world's greatest managers do.

How does this connect with career development and Appreciative Inquiry?

It connects because among the many findings, Buckingham and Coffman (1999) saw that success was linked to helping employees "become more of who he [sic] already is" (p. 141). Further, they said "Each person is different. Each person has a unique set of talents, and unique pattern of behaviors, of passions, of yearning. Each person's pattern of talents is enduring, resistant to change. Each person, therefore, has a unique destiny" (p. 141). Buckingham and Clifton (2001) built on that research to delineate the "strengths revolution at work" (p. 3). They wrote, "Faults and failings deserve study, but they reveal little about strengths. Strengths have their own pattern" (p. 3). They continued with the following statement:

> To excel in your chosen field and to find lasting satisfaction in doing so, you will need to understand your unique patterns. You will need to become expert at finding and describing and applying and practicing and refining your strengths. . . . Suspend whatever interest you may have in weakness and instead explore the intricate detail of your strengths. (pp. 3-4)

This led them to identifying 34 themes of talent which can be identified by using the StrengthsFinder Profile.

The distinction between Buckingham and

Clifton's (2001) approach and this Strength-Based Approach is seen most clearly in the process. The Strength-Based Approach, as delineated in this monograph, is based on the guided exploration by an individual of her or his experiences. The emerging themes are patterns that do not come from a predetermined list but are constructed by the individual. The difference is fitting one's exploration of experience to an existing list versus developing the list individually. The challenge in the former is figuring out what to do when the individual theme does not fit into the predetermined list. The challenge in the latter is that there are an infinite number of possible undefined categories or themes.

Both approaches are significant in their emphasis on increasing success and satisfaction by focusing on strengths and managing weaknesses.

Signature Strengths

Signature Strengths draws on empirical research in the field of Positive Psychology and "focuses on strengths rather than weaknesses, asserting that happiness is not the result of good genes or luck" (Adolescence, 2004, p. 838). This approach states that individuals are impacted by understanding their Signature Strengths. "Authentic happiness comes from identifying and cultivating your most fundamental strengths and using them every day in work, love, play, and parenting" (Seligman, 2002, p. xiii)

Peterson and Seligman (2004) believe that "character strengths are the bedrock of the human condition and that strength-congruent activity represents an important route to the psychological good life" (p. 4). There are 24 identified "signature strengths" which are combined into six virtues. The virtues are:

- Wisdom and knowledge — cognitive strengths that entail the acquisition and use of knowledge
- Courage — emotional strengths that involve the exercise of will to accomplish goals in the face of opposition, both external and internal
- Humanity — interpersonal strengths that involve "tending and befriending" others
- Justice — civic strengths that underlie healthy community life
- Temperance — strengths that protect against excess
- Transcendence — strengths that forge connections to the larger universe and provide meaning

(Summarized from Seligman, Steen, Park, & Peterson, 2005, p. 412)

With this approach, individuals take an assessment (available online) to receive a Values In Action (VIA) Signature Strengths report identifying the top five strengths to pay attention to and use more often.

The approach shared some similarities with that of Buckingham and Clifton (2001). Both approaches are based on research over the course of many years. While the research questions differed, the results supported a positive approach to career development. Both approaches were also similar in that each has a survey tool that is completed by individuals who then receive a personalized report that categorize their responses.

Positive Psychology is very similar to the Appreciative Inquiry approach as detailed here. Each approach discusses the necessity for a change in the way individuals view the world, and the power and influence of language. One distinction between the two is that one uses a static survey tool, the other uses a dynamic dialogue (the appreciative interview) as the data gathering instrument.

While there are several different approaches that draw on or suggest the use of and focus on strengths, the Strength-Based Approach to career development using Appreciative Inquiry offers a unique method to get to the desired goal. In each of the other assessments and approaches discussed, the focus is on identifying strengths so that they fit into a predetermined set of empirically generated strengths. The Appreciative Inquiry approach is focused on opening rather than narrowing strengths for the purpose of understanding and identifying.

Caveats

As with any approach, competence in the practice of educational or other types of interventions should be carefully considered. It is important to note that it is not recommended that this approach be employed in all situations and with every individual.

There are several caveats that are important to note:

1. This approach is not a tool but rather an approach, and it is not intended to fit every situation.
2. It requires that clients or participants are able to make observations about themselves, their behaviors, and the behaviors of others with respect to the focus of the inquiry.

3. It further requires that any potential language or communication barriers are prepared for in advance because the majority of the activities involve participant interaction.

4. Because this process draws heavily on dialogue with others through the Appreciative Inquiry interview, it is important to be clear with participants about the level of interaction and personal disclosure expectations that are necessary for this to be an effective interaction.

5. There is a cultural bias embedded in this approach: self-knowledge and understanding is important if growth and development is the goal. This is a value that is not necessarily true for all cultures.

6. An individual's behavior does not occur within a vacuum, and society's microsystems and macrosystems impact and contribute to making the achievement of women and people of color potentially more challenging (Cook, Heppner, & O'Brien, 2002). It is important that these influences are acknowledged and not discounted through the use of this approach.

7. It is possible that through the implementation of the Strength-Based Approach, clients, students, or participants may uncover more information or emotion than those using this approach are prepared to ethically and morally manage. It is incumbent upon the career development professional that she or he be prepared to make an appropriate referral to a qualified professional if needed.

8. It is the responsibility of the career development professional, teacher, or facilitator to be knowledgeable in career development theory and practice as well as knowledgeable in the Appreciative Inquiry approach.

It is also important to recognize the importance of an articulated contract between the career development professional and the client or student or participant. Due to the nature of the process discussed here, career development professionals need to be articulate and transparent about the process. The following is an excerpt of a communication that was sent in advance to every participant in a two-session Building on Your Strengths class:

Thank you for your interest in the *Building on Your Strengths* workshop. There have been some inquiries as to the nature of the workshop, so I thought it might be helpful to let you know in advance how the next two meetings will be focused. This email is sent in the interest of being transparent about the process so you can maximize your investment of time.

The workshop combines career development theory with Appreciative Inquiry (a systems tool applied to individual career development in this case). The process for the workshop draws on guided interviews and discussions with other members in the workshop. It is based on the following assumptions: individuals and systems have untapped rich stories; while some approaches identify fixes or deficits that need to be overcome, this process seeks that which is going right and builds on those strengths; language is seen as a powerful source for creating social reality; and conversations continually create new images that lead to new actions and behaviors.

Since this is a bit different than other approaches people have experienced, I want to be clear about what this is not. This workshop is not about utilizing any electronic/Web tools to key in an assessment which then suggests careers for you. It is also not about how to change your job classification or move up in a specific personnel system. It is also not connected to any commercial packages that are available.

If, after reading more about the workshop, it sounds like this will not fit your needs at this time, please feel free to cancel your registration or choose not to attend. The Adult and Student Services Center in the Division of Continuing Studies (http://www.dcs.wisc.edu/services/) does offer more specific opportunities to explore career development topics and would be a good resource for career assistance.

Thank you again for your interest. If you have any questions or have special needs that you would like to explore prior to the meeting, please feel free to let me know.

It is important for the implicit and explicit contract between the career development professional and the service user to be clear in advance. This early communication is respectful and demonstrates a level of professionalism that enhances any interaction.

Summary

This approach is about seeking and identifying those life-giving forces that are present when things are working well, when individuals are working at optimal levels. This approach leads to life-work satisfaction and success. It is also about capturing positive experiences and projecting them into the future through planning.

As a part of this process, each individual reflects on:

- the core factors that enable personal success
- the individual's story as it is being written, unfolding in the presence of a dialogue partner through the interview process
- the learning from experience as the individuals examine closely those moments when they have been at their best
- the most effective practices, strengths, and best qualities necessary to preserve the current situation as changes are made
- how a positive past — the best of experiences — can help the individual to be more daring and innovative when thinking about true potential
- the envisioned future including hopes and positive images
- building a life through positive and intentional planning that integrates the "best of who an individual is" with those with whom that individual shares her or his life

While there are some similarities between the Strength-Based Approach and other approaches using strengths, this approach encourages a change in the focus from a problem solving or deficit model to a positive perspective. This approach uses an interview process to initially gather personal information, and then uses structured learning activities to develop a plan for success. This experience is intended to find what works and to find ways to infuse more of the positive core into an individual's life and work. This journey encourages both the acceptance of a positive perspective as a world view (in contrast to a deficit-based view) and the development of language that supports a positive process for exploring an individual's career development needs.

Looking Ahead

The next chapter provides information about the Appreciative Inquiry process. Chapter III provides a practical example of the Strength-Based Approach in a classroom setting. The final chapter summarizes a broader perspective and areas to consider in the future.

II. An Appreciative Inquiry Primer

This chapter provides the necessary background and history of Appreciative Inquiry (AI). It is a summary of the literature and includes a detailed walk-through of the AI process from the powerful question to focusing interviews to creating provocative propositions.

What is Appreciative Inquiry?

Appreciative Inquiry is an organizational systems approach. This systems approach has great practical application to the field of career development, particularly as practitioners work with people who might have previously created a focus guided by fear, lack of self-knowledge, and immersion in a "half-empty" environment.

This chapter provides an overview of and background on Appreciative Inquiry, the five principles on which Appreciative Inquiry is based, the Appreciative Inquiry processes, and a description of the 4-D Cycle. While this chapter discusses Appreciative Inquiry as a systems approach, this monograph suggests that such a systems approach can be translated into individual terms and related directly to the career development process. The final two chapters demonstrate how that intersection occurs.

Defining Appreciative Inquiry

Watkins and Mohr (2001) provided a clear summary:

> Appreciative Inquiry is an approach to the development of human systems that recognizes that we can choose the view that either (1) Human systems are primarily constellations of problems/ obstacles to be analyzed and overcome, or (2) Human systems contain mysterious life-giving forces to be understood and embraced.
>
> Appreciative Inquiry recognizes that, whichever assumption we make about the nature of reality, the choice will lead to certain images being dominant in our minds, and those images will in turn lead to action at both the conscious and unconscious levels. (p. 61)

The position of this monograph is that career development can be approached either way, and that choosing the "life-giving forces" view provides greater opportunities for students and clients.

Hammond (1996) suggested that, in order to understand Appreciative Inquiry, it is important to understand the role of assumptions in organizations. "Organizations are made up of individuals who form groups to get work done. The groups behave according to the rules of group behavior. Assumptions are the set of beliefs shared by a group, that causes the group to think and act in certain ways" (p. 13). Hammond outlined assumptions of Appreciative Inquiry (as detailed in Chapter I). She provided an example contrasting the problem-solving model assumptions with the Appreciative Inquiry assumptions in response to the prompt "what did we do well in this meeting?" Hammond also suggested that most groups remain in the problem-solving model and:

> . . . apply the answers to the group's deficits. How can we do better as a result of what we didn't do well, is the underlying assumption for the problem-solving model.
>
> Contrast the appreciative mindset: We know that we have performed well at something (assumption 1) and need to explore how that happened and how to do more. Doing more of what works is the driver for Appreciative Inquiry as opposed [to] doing less of something we do not do well in the problem-solving model. In my experience, you cannot use Appreciative Inquiry as a questioning technique within the problem-solving model and achieve the desired result. For Appreciative Inquiry to work its magic, you have to believe and internalize the assumptions. That comes with study and practice. (Hammond, 1996, p. 23)

Embedded in this example is the view that the Appreciative Inquiry approach, if it is to be effective, needs to be accepted and integrated throughout the process. Choosing this perspective is at the heart of any Appreciative Inquiry.

As Appreciative Inquiry has evolved, so have the definitions. "The term 'appreciative' comes from the idea that when something increases in value it 'appreciates.' Therefore, Appreciative Inquiry focuses on the generative and life-giving forces in the system, the things we want to increase. By 'inquiry' we mean the process of seeking to understand through asking questions" (Watkins & Mohr, 2001, p. 14).

Watkins and Mohr also described Appreciative Inquiry as "a collaborative and highly participative, system-wide approach to seeking, identifying, and enhancing the 'life-giving' forces that are present when a system is performing optimally in human, economic, and organizational terms. It is a journey during which profound knowledge of a human system at its moments of wonder is uncovered and used to co-construct the best and highest future of that system" (p. 14).

Cooperrider, Whitney and Stavros (2005) provided a more detailed definition:

> Appreciative inquiry is the cooperative co-evolutionary search for the best in people, their organizations, and the world around them. It involves the discovery of what gives "life" to a living system when it is more effective, alive, and constructively capable in economic, ecological, and human terms. [In terms of the process,]
>
> AI involves the art and practice of asking questions that strengthen a system's capacity to apprehend, anticipate, and heighten positive potential. The inquiry is mobilized through the crafting of the "unconditional positive questions," often involving hundreds or thousands of people. AI interventions focus on the speed of imagination and innovation – instead of the negative, critical, and spiraling diagnoses commonly used in organizations. The discovery, dream, design, and destiny model links the energy of the positive core to changes never thought possible. (p. 3)

The commonalities in the definitions suggest that Appreciative Inquiry is an intentional, systems approach that focuses on and identifies the forces within the system that create vitality and energy. The goal in applying Appreciative Inquiry is to identify those vital forces and find ways to replicate them in both current situations and in the future. To remain consistent, an Appreciative Inquiry approach (in contrast to a tool or strategy) requires a broad application to every aspect of any intervention.

There are four propositions that underlie the practice of Appreciative Inquiry:

1. Inquiry into the "art of the possible" in organizational life should begin with appreciation.
2. Inquiry into what is possible should yield information that is applicable.

3. Inquiry into what is possible should be provocative.
4. Inquiry into the human potential of organizational life should be collaborative. (Cooperrider, Whitney and Stavros, 2005, p. 4)

The aforementioned definitions and the propositions have played a key role in developing the approach described here.

History

According to Watkins and Mohr (2001), "Appreciative Inquiry developed from a theory-building process used primarily by academics into a process for whole system change — but it still has theory-building (organization learning) at its core. Appreciative Inquiry enables organizations to build their own generative theory of enabling transformational shifts by learning from their most positively exceptional moment" (p. 15). Since the focus of this approach grew primarily out of organizations, Appreciative Inquiry initially was used in the area of organizational development work. Watkins and Mohr provide a very comprehensive history of Appreciative Inquiry; this list summarizes the highlights:

- 1980 — David Cooperrider performs a conventional diagnosis and organizational analysis for the Cleveland Clinic Project, resulting in an analysis of factors contributing to the highly effective functioning of the clinic. Appreciative Inquiry is referenced in a footnote on a report of emergent themes. This sets the stage for the first articulation of the theory and practice of Appreciative Inquiry and becomes the topic of Cooperrider's dissertation.

- 1986 — Cooperrider completes his doctoral dissertation, which lays out the principles and phases of Appreciative Inquiry and provides a social constructionist meta-theory that moves beyond a deficit or problem focus.

- 1987 — For the first time, the Appreciative Inquiry approach appears in a professional publication; Appreciative Inquiry moves beyond theory to an intervention framework; the first public Appreciative Inquiry workshop held in San Francisco.

- 1980s and 1990s — Appreciative Inquiry is the focus of discussions at multiple large events, and a number of centers and institutes related to Appreciative Inquiry are founded.

- 1990 — The U.S. Agency for International Development selects Case Western Reserve as their university partner in the Organizational Excellence Program (OEP) pilot. OEP later becomes the Global Excellence in Management initiative (GEM), which serves as a laboratory for creating approaches and models. It also fosters major innovative ways to use Appreciative Inquiry, which has expanded to international audiences.
- 1992 — Imagine Chicago uses an Appreciative Inquiry approach in community development efforts in which children conduct hundreds of appreciative interviews with adults throughout the city.
- 1996 — *The Thin Book of Appreciative Inquiry* (Hammond, 1996) is widely-distributed and serves as the basic introductory book for Appreciative Inquiry
  (adapted from Watkins & Mohr, 2001, pp. 15-21).

The history of Appreciative Inquiry continued as the approach found international acceptance at meetings, through work with the Dalai Lama, at numerous symposia, and with the launch of the European Appreciative Inquiry network. In 2005, the comprehensive *Appreciative Inquiry Handbook* (Cooperrider, Whitney, & Stavros, 2005) was published as a workbook for leaders of change.

The Five Principles of Appreciative Inquiry

There are five principles which inspired and strengthened Appreciative Inquiry. These principles moved the foundation of Appreciative Inquiry to a theory of change and also guided it from theory to practice. The principles are (a) the Constructionist Principle, (b) the Principle of Simultaneity, (c) the Poetic Principle, (d) the Anticipatory Principle, and (e) the Positive Principle. Each will be described briefly here. Cooperrider & Whitney (2000) and Cooperrider, Whitney, and Stavros (2005) provide more detailed descriptions of these principles.

The Constructionist Principle

The Constructionist Principle is based on the idea that knowing is at the center of every attempt to change

and that the way we come to know something is important to both our understanding of how change occurs and our ability to sustain change over time. This principle implies that the topics of inquiry are the products of social processes.

Cooperrider and Whitney (2000) described the purpose of inquiry "as totally inseparable and intertwined with action … not so much mappings or explanations of yesterday's world, but anticipatory articulations of tomorrow's possibilities" (p. 18). They continued, "Constructionism, because of its emphasis on the communal basis of knowledge and its radical questioning of everything that is taken-for-granted as the 'objective' or seemingly immutable, invites us to find ways to increase the generative capacity of knowledge" (p. 18).

Cooperrider & Whitney (2000) highlighted the important contribution of this principle:

> At stake are questions that pertain to the deepest dimensions of our being and humanity; how we know what we know, whose voices and interpretations matter, whether the world is governed by external laws independent of human choices and consciousness, and where is knowledge to be located (in the individual "mind", or out there "externally" in nature or impersonal structures)? (p.17)

It is important to understand how organizations come to "know what we know," and how that influences the organization's abilities to imagine the future. The same can be said in applying this principle to individuals.

Cooperrider and Whitney (2000) provided a good summary of Constructionism by describing it as "built around a keen appreciation of the power of language and discourse of all types (from words to metaphors to narrative forms, etc.) to create our sense of reality — our sense of the true, the good, the possible" (p. 17). The notion of understanding how organizations understand who they are, the implication of that knowledge on the vision for the possibilities for the future of that organization, and the ability to react and respond based on that knowledge, demonstrates the important contribution the Constructionist Principle has made in the development of Appreciative Inquiry.

The Principle of Simultaneity

The term "simultaneity" implies that more than one thing is happening at a time. In this case, it relates to the idea that:

> . . . inquiry and change are not truly separate moments; they can and should be simultaneous.

Inquiry is intervention. The seeds of change are the things people think and talk about, the things people discover and learn, and the things that inform dialogue and inspire images of the future. They are implicit in the very first questions asked" (Cooperrider, Whitney, & Stavros, 2005, p. 8).

Cooperrider and Whitney (2000) also stated that "[t]he questions we ask set the stage for what we 'find,' and what we 'discover' (the data) becomes the linguistic material, the stories, out of which the future is conceived, conversed about, and constructed" (p. 18). The Simultaneity Principle builds on the importance of understanding the origin of knowledge and impact of language presented by the Constructionist Principle, and moves to the forefront the importance of recognizing that asking questions can be simultaneously data gathering and directing the course of the discussion.

The Poetic Principle

The Poetic Principle captures the idea that just as a good book, movie, or poem is open to interpretation, so are the actions (past and present) of organizations. Following that premise, the Poetic Principle suggests that:

- An organization's story is constantly being co-authored.
- Reconsideration of aims and focus of any inquiry in the domain of change management is important.
- Topics move in the direction of our attention.
- Past, present, and futures are endless sources of learning, inspiration, or interpretation.
- Moments of creativity and innovation or moments of debilitating bureaucratic stress can be chosen as topics to study.
- What is chosen then directs attention, energy and resources toward the topic.

(summarized from Cooperrider, Whitney, & Stavros, 2005, pp. 8–9)

The Anticipatory Principle

Watkins and Mohr (2001) captured the essence of the Anticipatory Principle: "In myriad of ways ranging from physiological responses at the individual level to the creation of new strategies and organizational architectures, we collectively create the very future that we anticipate" (p. 32). Cooperrider, Whitney, and Stavros (2005) stated that "the anticipatory view of organizational life is that the image of the future guides what

might be called the current behavior of any organism or organization" (p. 9). They continued later, "Organizations exist . . . because people who govern and maintain them share some sort of discourse or projection about what the organization is, how it will function, what it will achieve, and what will likely become" (p. 9).

The idea that "what is expected is often realized" is the foundation of this principle. Again, Watkins and Mohr (2001) provided a summary of this implication:

This *view of how we shape our future* gives us a whole new way of understanding the process of change in an organization. Rather than being limited to the traditional view of change as an event that has a beginning, middle, and end ... we now see change as a continuous process, ongoing in every conversation we have, in every inquiry we make, in every action we take to 'know' or understand something about our organization and/or the about the world. (pp. 32-33)

The implication, then, is that if something different is expected, it is possible that something different will occur.

The Positive Principle

The Positive Principle promotes the value of the positive image and how that image creates thought patterns and ultimately affirming behaviors.

This principle connects back to the literature on positive psychology as discussed in Chapter 1. It was also included because of the extensive experience the creators had with this principle, as seen in this excerpt from Cooperrider and Whitney (2000):

It grows out of years of experience with appreciative inquiry. Put most simply, it has been our experience that building and sustaining momentum for change requires large amounts of positive affect and social bonding — things like hope, excitement, inspiration, caring, camaraderie, sense of urgent purpose, and sheer joy in creating something meaningful together. What we found is that the more positive the question we ask in our work the more long lasting and successful the change effect. It does not help, we have found, to begin our inquiries from the standpoint of the world as a problem to be solved. We are more effective the longer we can retain the spirit of inquiry of the everlasting beginner. The major thing we do that makes the difference is to craft and seed, in better and more catalytic ways, the unconditional positive question. (p. 20)

These are the five principles on which Appreciative Inquiry is founded. Each organization faces many choices. One choice is to take a positive and more affirming approach to organizational development by identifying the strengths and life-giving forces. The strengths and life-giving forces are then used to create images of the future that are sustainable and enduring. These principles are also the foundation for the 4-D Cycle discussed briefly in this chapter and in greater detail in Chapter III.

The Appreciative Approach Processes and the 4-D Cycle

In addition to the five principles introduced in this chapter, there are five processes that are part of an Appreciative Inquiry:

1. Choose the positive as the focus of inquiry.
2. Inquire into stories of life-giving forces.
3. Locate themes that appear in the stories and select topics for further inquiry.
4. Create shared images for a preferred future.
5. Find innovative ways to create that future.
(Adapted from Watkins & Mohr, 2001, p. 40)

For the purposes of this monograph, and the application of Appreciative Inquiry to individual career development, the processes have been slightly modified as seen in Chapter I.

Watkins and Mohr (2005) described these as generic processes, with the term "generic" intentionally used to underscore the flexibility and likely overlaps among these processes: "They [the generic processes] overlap and repeat themselves without predictability, which is another reason that … [one] must be grounded in the theory, research, and principles of AI … [when] translating these generic processes into practice" (p. 39).

There are a number of different models which describe the phases or stages used in Appreciative Inquiry. For the purposes of this monograph, the 4-D Cycle presented in Cooperrider, Whitney, and Stavros (2005) was used to build the Strength-Based Approach to career development.

The 4-D Cycle

The 4-D Cycle is a model that demonstrates the phased process through which the appreciative intervention progresses when Appreciative Inquiry is applied in an organizational setting. There are four phases in the Appreciative Inquiry 4-D Cycle through which an orga-

nization progresses: (a) discovery, (b) dream, (c) design, and (d) destiny. While the model is delineated into four phases, there is actually a step before an appreciative intervention moves into the first phase. Prior to the discovery phase of the 4-D Cycle, "an Affirmative Topic must be chosen to focus the inquiry. The topic choice is so important because it directs the focus for the rest of the intervention. Therefore, the right topics need to be created or chosen. These topics will ultimately guide the formulation of questions" (Cooperrider, Whitney, & Stavros, 2005, p. 29). Examples of affirmative topics might include exceptional service in every contact, or leadership at all levels, or every employee feels valued. This choosing of the positive is also seen as making an "Affirmative Topic Choice" prior to any activity in the four phases.

The discovery phase asks the question, "What gives life?", seeking to find the best of what is. It is also described as the appreciating phase. The dream phase is seen as the envisioning phase and centers on "What might be," seeking to imagine what the world is calling for. The third phase, design, asks "How can it be?" which leads determining what is the ideal. Co-constructing is the task in this phase. Sustaining, or asking "What will be?" is the focus of the destiny phase. It is about how to empower, learn, and adjust/improvise (Cooperrider, Whitney, & Stavros, 2005 p. 30). In Appreciative Inquiry, that learning process is centered on organizational learning; in career development, the learning is at the individual level.

The 4-D Cycle is discussed in much greater detail in Chapter III.

The Positive Core

The positive core is that which "makes up the best of an organization and its people" (Cooperrider, Whitney, & Stavros, 2005, p. 419). While distinct from the 4-D Cycle, the positive core is woven throughout the Appreciative Inquiry (AI) process:

AI has demonstrated that human systems grow in the direction of their persistent inquiries, and this propensity is strongest and most sustainable when the means and ends of the inquiry are positively correlated. In the AI process, the future is consciously constructed upon the positive core strengths of the organization. Linking the energy of this core directly to any change agenda suddenly and democratically creates and mobilizes topics never before thought possible. (Cooperrider, Whitney, Stavros, 2005, p. 30).

The Appreciative Interview

The appreciative interview is defined as "an interview that uncovers what gives life to an organization, department, or community when at its best" (Cooperrider, Whitney, & Stavros, 2005, p. 415). The purpose of the appreciative interview is to gather data. As mentioned earlier in the chapter, the questions that are asked in the appreciative interview are critical to the direction of the inquiry. The appreciative interview is usually steered by the interview guide, which has been very carefully constructed by the interview guide team and is typically based around variations of four questions. Watkins and Mohr (2001) provide samples of four generic questions used with organizations from which an interview guide might be developed:

1. *Best Experience:* Tell me about the best times that you have had with your organization. Looking at your entire experience, recall a time when you felt most alive, most involved, or most excited about your involvement. What made it an exciting experience? Who was involved? Describe the event in detail.
2. *Values:* What are the things you value deeply; specifically, the things you value about yourself, your work, and your organization.
3. *Core Life-Giving Factor or Value:* What do you think is the core life-giving factor or value of your organization? What is it that, if it did not exist, would make your organization totally different than it currently is?
4. *Three Wishes:* If you had three wishes for this organization, what would they be?
   (Abbreviated from Watkins & Mohr, 2001, p. 84)

Cooperrider, Whitney, & Stavros (2005) identified several key components to appreciative interviews: assumption of health and vitality; connection through empathy; personal excitement; commitment, and caring; intense focus through "third ear" and "third eye;" generative questioning, cueing and guiding; and moving from monologue to dialogue (p. 97).

When conducting an appreciative interview, it is important to describe the process before the first interview. In addition, it is important when working with people in organizations to give them a sense for what to expect. Cooperrider, Whitney, & Stavros (2005) offered these tips to suggest to participants when conducting an organizational appreciative interview:

- Explain Appreciative Inquiry
- Respect anonymity
- Manage the negatives — working toward the positive
- Start with specific stories — getting into the interview rhythm
- Generalize about life-giving forces
- Listen for themes and life-giving factors
- Keep track of the time
- Have fun and be yourself
  (Abridged from Cooperrider, Whitney, & Stavros, 2005, pp 95–97)

In summary, the appreciative interview elicits information or data. It is a process which is treated by the Appreciative Inquiry planning facilitator as action research that attempts to discover the best of what is in the organization or system. The meaning of the data "is drawn from the foundation of dialogues that inspires the dreams based on the best stories told (continuity) and the best of what will come (novelty). The Design and Destiny phases transform (transition) the data into the desired future" (Cooperrider, Whitney, & Stavros, 2005, p. 98). Once the data is collected, the goal shifts to reducing the information for interpretation, then testing the themes through dialogue to ensure the interviewee's meanings are represented in the final results.

Conclusion

In the broadest sense, the Appreciative Inquiry process "involves [a process of] interviewing and storytelling to draw out the best of the past and set the stage for effective visualization of the future" (Cooperrider, Whitney, & Stavros, 2005, p. 4). Watkins and Mohr (2001) described Appreciative Inquiry as:

An alternative theory of organizational intervention [that] would suggest that a fundamental pre-condition for all organization change work ... is to shift the flow of "issue framing dialogues" in the direction of health rather than pathology in order to shift the flow of dialogue from an analysis of malfunction to a holistic understanding of moments of optimal performance. The choice to focus on moments of optimal performance and our conscious use of inquiry are powerful interventions in and of themselves. (p. 33)

Cooperrider, Whitney and Stavros (2005) expressed great hope for Appreciative Inquiry: "We may have reached the end of problem solving. AI is a powerful approach to transformation as a mode of inquiry capable of inspiring, mobilizing, and sustaining human system change. The future of OD [Organizational Development] belongs, instead, to methods that affirm, compel, and accelerate anticipatory learning involving larger and larger levels of collectivity" (p. 2).

Appreciative Inquiry is an organizational system approach that looks at the best of what is, develops an image of that success, and projects that image into hopes and wishes for the future. While focused initially on the change process in organizations, the development of the approach and its processes offer new insights and opportunities when possible transferable concepts are considered relative to the career development process. Applying this approach and processes to the career development process is the focus of the final two chapters in this monograph.

III. Appreciative Inquiry and Career Development

This chapter provides an in-depth discussion of each of the process points (appreciating, envisioning, co-constructing, and sustaining) with definitions. The notion of managing weaknesses is also introduced and discussed using the Appreciative Inquiry concepts. Activities that demonstrate possible individual and group interventions at a practical level are included.

The 4-D Cycle: Discovery, Dream, Design, and Destiny

Before entering the four phases of the 4-D Cycle, an Affirmative Topic must be chosen. The Affirmative Topic is followed by the discovery phase where appreciating and valuing are the actions, then the dream phase where envisioning is the action. The third phase, design, consists of co-constructing the future and, finally, the destiny phase is where learning, empowering and improvising to sustain the future are the actions taken (Cooperrider, Whitney, & Stavros, 2005, p.5). Figure 1 depicts the Strength-Based Approach Cycle, integrating career development concepts of "who am I?," "where am I going?," "how do I get there?" with the phases of the 4-D Cycle.

In this chapter, a six-hour career development workshop focusing on using Appreciative Inquiry in a career development learning event will serve as the example integrating the 4-D Cycle with career development. To deliver this workshop, it would be judicious for the facilitator to have strong facilitation and/or counseling skills. The workshop components (including activities) will be used to demonstrate how this application can occur.

Figure 1. Strength-Based Approach Cycle

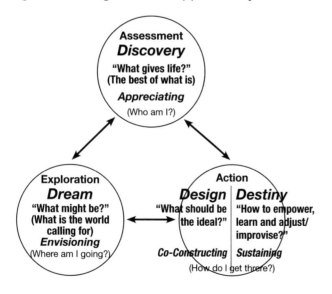

Selecting an Affirmative Topic

Affirmative Topic choice is defined as "the topics identified in the Discovery phase that guide the formation of the interview guide. It is a positive descriptive phrase representing the organization's focus for change" (Cooperrider, Whitney, & Stavros, 2005, p. 415). When applied to career development, it remains a positive descriptive phrase representing the individual's focus for change. Choosing the topic is critical because it directs the rest of the process. The nature of the topic and how it is delineated is also important in taking deficit issues and transforming them into affirmative topics.

Cooperrider, Whitney, and Stavros (2005) set the stage for this pre-first phase step:

> AI is deliberate in its life-centric search. … The art of appreciation is the art of discovering and valuing those factors that give life to a group or an organization. The process involves interviewing and storytelling to draw out the best of the past and set the state for effective visualization of the future. (pp. 3-4)

When moving from the organizational perspective (where Appreciative Inquiry is in its purest form) to the individual career development perspective (the Strength-Based Approach), this description would change from

> "The art of appreciation is the art of discovering and valuing those factors that give life to a **group or an organization.**"

to

> "The art of appreciation is the art of discovering and valuing those factors that give life to the **individual.**"

There is great transferability between the contexts (organizational and individual).

In the organizational approach, the process of selecting a topic begins with a topic selection team. This team is typically a small group of people representing different areas of the organization who go through a mini-appreciative interview process. Four foundational questions are explored in small subgroups, ideally in pairs:

1. What was a peak experience or "high point"?
2. What are the things valued most about
   a. yourself?
   b. the nature of your work?
   c. your organization?
3. What are the core factors that "give life" to organizing?
4. What are the three wishes to heighten vitality and health?
   (Cooperrider, Whitney, & Stavros, 2005, p. 36)

In a workplace, the topic selection team might be work groups or committees who convene to discuss the growth and development of the workforce team and are guided by the four questions.

Once the mini-appreciative interview process is complete, the topic selection team reconvenes to dialog (focusing on listening and understanding) and deliberate. This is one of the most important moments in the process. Where, in some situations, lengthy discussions over single words seem like an unproductive use of time, in the Appreciative Inquiry process each word is critical and should be thought through very carefully. The critical nature of the language chosen connects back to the Constructionist Principle (that stated that the way that we come to know something is important to both our understanding of how change occurs and how to sustain change over time) discussed in Chapter II.

In the end, no more than five Affirmative Topics should be identified and the topics should meet these criteria:

- Topics are affirmative or stated in the positive.
- Topics are desirable. They identify the career objectives people want.
- The group is genuinely curious about the topic and wants to learn more.
- The topics move in the direction the group wants to go.
  (Cooperrider, Whitney, & Stavros, 2005, p. 37)

These four criteria are transformed when applied to the career development process. The transformed criteria are:

- Topic(s) is affirmative or stated in the positive.

- Topic(s) is desirable and personally meaningful. It identifies the objectives the individual wants.
- The individual is genuinely curious about her or his direction and wants to learn more.
- The topic(s) moves in the direction the individual wants to go.

Using the career workshop example, the Affirmative Topic was chosen in advance and used to do the marketing for the workshop. Since the process is focused on assisting the individual, the Affirmative Topic was "Create an action plan that honors your strengths and articulates your hopes for your future." In this case, the Affirmative Topic choice was agreed upon by each participant since they chose to register once the topic was identified.

Choosing the Affirmative Topic is critical to the appreciative interview guide, and is central to the process.

What Gives Life?
The Discovery Phase

In this phase, the focus is on the discovery of the life-giving forces. During this phase, the process begins to build the positive core. It focuses on uncovering and valuing the best of "what is?" or the best of what is happening in the individual's current situation. The information builds on the Affirmative Topic Choice through engagement in the appreciative interviews (Cooperrider, Whitney, & Stavros, 2005, p. 416).

The Building on Your Strengths *Interview Guide* demonstrates an interview with a partner. The purpose in having this in an interactive interview format is twofold: it allows the participant to respond to interviews without also having to seek out themes and patterns (since that is the role of the partner), and it allows participants to hear firsthand how others have been successful and what strategies have worked. See Appendix B, Activity 1 for a detailed description of the activity, which is comprised of four areas:

1. Let's begin by talking about a time when you felt most happy in your career — a time when you were having fun and doing a great job. Describe the situation. Explore these areas with your partner.
   a. What was it that created a sense of happiness and fulfillment?
   b. Who was involved? What did the other person(s) do?
   c. What did you do that contributed to

your own sense of happiness and fulfillment?

    d. As you think about that time when you felt most happy, what workplace characteristics stand out for you as important or necessary for your happiness and success?

    e. What about the experience made it meaningful?

2. There are often times in our lives when we feel particularly energized and positive. Looking at your life experiences, can you recall a peak work or learning experience when you felt most alive, most involved, or most excited about your work? Explore these areas.

    a. What made it an exciting experience?

    b. Who were the significant others in the experience?

    c. Why were they significant?

    d. What was it about you that made it a peak experience?

    e. What were the most important factors in the work that helped to make it a peak experience? (Examples might be relationships, leadership, resources, etc.)

3. Let's talk for a moment about the things that you value deeply — specifically, the aspects you value about yourself, the nature of your work, and the work environment.

    a. Without being humble, what do you value the most about yourself as a human being, a friend, a parent, a citizen, or a son/daughter?

    b. When you are feeling best about your work, what do you value about the task itself?

    c. What about the workplace do you value most?

    d. What is the single most important thing that your work has contributed to your life?

4. If you had three wishes for your career, what would they be? Please list in order of priority.

    Wish One:
    Wish Two:
    Wish Three:

To begin to collect the data from the appreciative interview, the interviewer takes notes and completes a summary sheet which is shared with the interviewee. The framing questions for that summary sheet dialogue are

1. What did you hear the person describing in the interview as life-giving forces?

2. Identify three to five major themes or patterns that emerged from the interview.

3. What were the most quotable statements that came from your conversation?

4. Please summarize what you heard, felt, or saw as the interviewee's strengths.

The identification of themes is important. A theme, according to Watkins and Mohr (2001), "is an idea or concept about what is present in the stories that people report are the times of greatest excitement, creativity, and reward" (p.119). They continue, "For example, in many stories you may hear that when the topic covered by the question is at its best, people report a 'feeling of success,' or 'clarity about purpose' or 'fun and excitement.' These phrases are 'themes'" (p. 119). These themes also connect back to Super's notion of career self concept (Super, Savickas, and Super, 1996) discussed in Chapter I. In addition to the appreciative interview, there is a guided imagery activity that taps into the discovery phase in the career development workshop.

The guided imagery activity (see Activity 2 in Appendix B) centers on life in the future, and draws on the themes from the appreciative interview. It is not done in pairs, but is directed by a facilitator. It is, in a sense, a bridging activity to guide the transition between this phase and the dream phase. The following excerpt provides a glimpse into the imagery activity:

Imagine those themes have been implemented fully in your everyday life and work. Imagine that those life experiences from the past are now the typical, everyday experiences in your life. Your life is full of images, feelings, and conversations representing those positive themes and patterns.

We are now going to travel ahead to your future. Put yourself three years ahead into the future. Imagine that your day is just beginning and you are preparing for work. You are energized and eager to begin your day because you know you will be spending your day doing work that draws on your strengths and provides you with great satisfaction. As you look around, you see the world just as you hoped it would be. What do you see? Picture in your mind what is happening.

Who is around you? How is the world different? As you imagine your day ahead, what pictures emerge that continue to provide you with energy and enthusiasm. How does it feel to see those pictures?

You begin to reflect back to the journey you have been on over the past three years. How did this come about? What helped it to happen? What are the things that supported this journey? Who did you draw on for support in your success? What makes this vision so compelling to you?

Consider how quickly you got to where you are. How were you able to realize this vision with such unsurpassed speed? As you remember your progress, you feel really good about creating such a healthy and meaningful change in your work and in your life.

To complete this activity, there is a processing sheet that captures the images and feelings elicited by the guided imagery:

- Following the guided-imagery activity, please jot down the first few words that capture the images, feelings and reactions to your experience.

- What are you "meant" or "called" to do?

- What is the inspiration that supports you?

These two activities initiate the process of appreciating what one has, the best of what is, and the positive core and projects the process into the future, carrying forward the best. The next phase is the dream phase, where the positive core identified in the discovery phase is amplified.

What Might Be? The Dream Phase

This phase is characterized by participant dialogue, and the creation of the dream. The difference between the career development approach and the Appreciative Inquiry approach in this area is that, again, the focus is on the individual rather than the organization. This phase is identified with the question "what might be?" (Cooperrider, Whitney, & Stavros, 2005, p. 417). The dream phase was also described as the time for "people to listen carefully to moments of organizational life at its best and to share images of their hopes and dreams for their collective future" (Cooperrider & Whitney, 2005, p.27).

Returning to the career development workshop example, in the dream phase participants are asked to begin to identify the recurring themes and patterns they noticed from the *Building on Your Strengths* interview (and the dialogue that followed) and from the guided imagery activity (Activity 3 in Appendix B). The dialogue is structured with these questions:

- What are the root causes of your success? What themes or patterns are at the heart of peak experiences and wishes for the future?

- Were any vital life themes or values overlooked in the stories or the guided imagery?

- What are the most engaging and exciting possibilities for you as you think about your future life and work?

Note the reversal of language in the first question. How often do people discuss the root causes of the problem? This shift in language represents the ever-present focus on the positive in the Strength-Based Approach.

The next dream phase activity, titled "Creating My Ideal Work-Life Scenario" (Appendix B, Activity 4), is directly related to answering the question "what might be?" Participants are asked to respond to four statements. The lead into the activity is

Capture the engaging and exciting positive possibilities by creating your "Ideal Work-Life Scenario." Let's begin by drawing together the different pieces. Please try to write your responses in the present tense, and be sure it is positive, uses energizing language, and is bold and provocative.

The second part of the direction highlights an important component — language is seen as a powerful source for creating reality — so the language in this activity needs to be positive and energizing. This ensures against negative language based on deficits such as "I will not" or "I will avoid."

The four statements are:

- The best work situation for me is one where I …

- The most important life giving forces that I need to carry forward are …

- My ideal work-life scenario would be…

- My ideal position gives me energy and a feeling of purpose because …

Completion of this activity positions the participant to move into the next phase, the design phase.

What Should Be the Ideal?
The Design Phase

The design phase focuses on co-constructing the future with those who are important to the participant. This is also the phase where the "provocative proposition" is created by determining the idea. Provocative propositions "embody the organizational dream in the ongoing activities. Everything about organizing is reflected and responsive to the dream, the organization's greatest potential" (Cooperrider, Whitney, & Stavros, 2005, p. 40). Hammond (1996) described the purpose of provocative propositions as "keep[ing] our best at a conscious level" (p. 39). She continued,

> They are symbolic because they have meaning well beyond words, reminding us of what is best about the organization and how everyone can participate in creating more of the best. Provocative propositions are derived from stories that actually took place in an organization. This grounding in history, tradition, and facts distinguishes Appreciative Inquiry form other visioning methods in which dreams serve as the primary basis for the vision. (p. 39)

An example of a career development provocative proposition might be

> My whole life I have been interested in writing poetry, and I was very successful when I was younger. I am now at the point in my life where I have successfully raised three children who are off raising families of their own, My interest in poetry has been reignited, and I am motivated to pursue my dreams. I am going to write two poetry pieces a month and enter the three largest poetry contests in the United States, I will also begin submitting pieces to *Poetry* magazine.

The progression in the career development workshop example moves participants from an activity focused on innovating possibilities, to prioritizing, to the provocative proposition concentrated on a "will do" goal which serves as the provocative proposition statement for the Strength-Based Approach.

In reacting to the Ideal Work-life Scenario, participants in the "Innovative Ways to Create the Future: My Sequence for Success" (Activity 5 in Appendix B) are asked to brainstorm in two different areas:

- What could you change, adapt, or adopt in your current situation to get a sense of purpose and energy through your ideal position?

- If you were to be TEN TIMES MORE BOLD in the pursuit of your ideal work-life scenario, what would you do?

These two areas lead to a prioritizing activity called "Shoulds, Wants, and Will" (Activity 6 in Appendix B). Participants are asked to identify five activities or behaviors (in positive language) that they feel they should do, which is then reduced to three things (from the initial list) that they want to do, leading to one action that they will take. That single remaining action is transformed into the provocative proposition in the "Action Plan: My WILL DO Goal" activity (Activity 7 in Appendix B).

The "Action Plan: My WILL DO Goal" activity guides the participant through a planning process, including an evaluation of the action steps, modified from Cooperrider, Whitney, & Stavros (2005). It is intended that each action goal will receive an affirmative response to the following questions:

- Is it a "yes-able" idea (are you likely to get support from the important actors in your life)?
- Does it address/reflect the underlying principles in your positive possibilities statement?
- What are you already doing (key success factors) that can be continued or enhanced?
- What new actions would create an impact? (p. 140)

The responses to these questions guide the development of the plan. An example, if there is not any support from the important actors in a person's life, then finding a support network would need to be integrated into the plan.

This activity crosses into the destiny phase as it is the start of action planning and commitments. Once the goal is stated, the next steps include identifying the sequence necessary for that goal to be achieved, and identifying any small steps that might have the greatest impact.

How to Empower, Learn, and Adjust/Improvise?
The Destiny Phase

The destiny phase is guided by the preferred future and is defined by "how can it be?" It picks up at action planning and follows through to commitments. "The key to sustaining the momentum is to build an 'appreciative eye' into all of the organization's systems, procedures, and ways of working" (Cooperrider, Whitney, & Stavros, 2005, p. 41).

When applied to career development, this phase is about cultivating and sustaining the plans that have been created. The process for moving from the design phase to the destiny phase is:

1. For each of the goals, identify two or three action steps necessary to get that goal moving and heading in the right direction.
2. Identify the goals and action steps that draw on strengths, life-giving forces, and wishes. Also, identify those goals that will require drawing on the larger support system.
3. Identify which of the goals and action steps that something can be done about and that are within the participant's ability to influence the outcome.
4. What is the smallest step (an action, a decision, a behavior) that could be taken that would have the largest impact?

The final step in this process is to identify any "Possible Bumps in the Road to Building on My Strengths" (Activity 8 in Appendix B).

This process asks participants to identify any bumps or obstacles that need to be managed. These could include social, economic, or other factors. Buckingham and Clifton (2001) coined a phrase *"to capitalize on your strengths,* whatever they may be, and *manage around your weaknesses,* whatever they may be" (p. 27). In the final planning stages, it is important to consider what the bumps are that may slow participants down. The choice of the word "bump" was intentionally chosen (as most words in an appreciative approach are), in contrast to obstacle or block, to indicate that this is not something that will stop implementation, but an indicator to address. The choices provided to participants once these bumps are identified are: ignore, respond, or respond later.

To assist participants in sustaining the action plan, participants are reminded of the Affirmative Topic Choice as laid out in the goals in this way:

> In addition to developing your life-work plan, the goal of this process is to create and enhance your ability to choose a positive focus in your career development inquiries, continuously reflect on your strengths, react to changing circumstances using your "life-giving forces" as a guide, and respond in ways that challenge you and provoke creative responses leading to the successful realization of your future vision for your career and life.

Also provided are the identified competencies that may lead to greater progress in productivity, efficiency, and performance (modified from Cooperrider, Whitney, & Stavros, 2005) including:

- Affirmative Competence, which involves the capacity to appreciate positive possibilities by selectively focusing on current and past strengths, successes, and potentials
- Expansive Competence, which is the ability to challenge personal comfort zones — including but not limited to personal habits and conventional practices — by asking how to be more bold, and by prioritizing efforts not by how easy they are to accomplish, but rather how much the effort contributes to the positive core and life-giving forces.
- Generative Competence, which encourages understanding in how the results of personal actions contribute to a meaningful purpose for the individual and society, and to recognize how to understand and experience a sense of progress
- Collaborative Competence, which is the intentional engagement of the important actors in life in ongoing dialogue about those things valued most deeply, including how to seek out diverse perspectives to continuously transform your self-image and future possibilities
  (pp. 181-182)

The end of this process does not indicate the end of the career development process.

While the term "destiny" is used to depict this phase, in the organizational use "the Destiny phase is ongoing and brings the organization back, full circle, to the Discovery phase. In a systemic fashion, continued appreciative inquiry may result in new affirmative topic choices, continuous dialogues, and continued learning" (Cooperrider, Whitney, & Stavros, 2005, p. 41).

This is also true in the career development process where ongoing learning and discovery is depicted in the three circles in Figure 1 at the beginning of the chapter. The three circles symbolize the type of developmental progression that individuals face when handling career-related development tasks "in such a way as to become the kind of person he or she wants to be" (Super, Savickas, and Super, 1996, p. 140). The circles all connect back with each other indicating movement forward and backward as needed to meet the ever-changing needs of participants.

Summary

In Appreciative Inquiry, the 4-D Cycle, consisting of the Affirmative Topic Choice and the four phases (discovery, dream, design, and destiny), serves as one model for understanding and implementing an appreciative approach. The transferability of this organizational, systems approach to career development is quite simple. The phases link to the career development processes of "who am I?", "where am I going?", and "how do I get there?" This chapter expanded on the 4-D Cycle and its application to career development through the Strengths-Based approach. The activities taken from a career development workshop delineated each of the phases (including topic choice) of the 4-D model, demonstrating the applicability and effectiveness of integrating Appreciative Inquiry approach with career development.

The final chapter details further the relationship of the Strength-Based Approach to career development, along with additional resources and suggestions for implementation.

IV. Implementing a Strength-Based Approach

This chapter suggests ways in which the Strength-Based Approach can be implemented. Included are materials to deliver a Strength-Based Approach workshop. Web sites and other resources are also identified. The final section of this chapter serves as the conclusion to the monograph.

Implementing a Strength-Based Approach to Career Development

The Strength-Based Approach to career development focuses on discovering the best in people and in the relevant world around them. It is the art and practice of asking unconditionally positive questions that strengthen an individual's capacity to comprehend, anticipate, and heighten positive potential. Instead of negation, criticism and a diagnosis, there is discovery, dream, design, and destiny.

The Strength-Based Approach emphasizes identifying and replicating the positive core. It links the energy of the positive core directly to the change agenda so that changes the individual never thought possible are mobilized toward life-enhancing forces and an energized action plan. It looks at the best of "what is" to develop images of success and satisfaction, and projects those images into hopes and wishes for the future. This definition draws on and is modified from Cooperrider, Whitney, and Stavros (2005) and Watkins and Mohr (2001).

The Strength-Based Approach is consistent with most career development theoretical perspectives and may help operationalize or expand constructs (e.g., positive regard, and career-related developmental tasks and activities). The goal of a Strength-Based Approach is to create an action plan that honors an individual's strengths and articulates her or his hopes for the future. Success is realized by the progression through the Strength-Based Approach Cycle which occurs in three phases, from discovery to dream to design/destiny, as discussed in Chapter III.

The Strength-Based Approach is intended for individuals who are seeking to explore career and life planning issues through face-to-face counseling, small-group educational experiences, or through workshops or courses. It is not intended to discount life experiences such as discrimination, harassment, or abuse of any nature, which may transcend the Strength-Based Approach and which should be taken seriously.

Likewise, the Strength-Based Approach does not serve as a substitute perspective for people who are suffering and need the assistance of qualified physical and mental health professionals. It is possible that through the activities suggested in this monograph, individuals might be reconnected with an intensity of emotion for which those using this approach are not prepared to adequately or appropriately address. This may not be the most effective approach for every individual. Practitioners should be aware of many different techniques, models, and approaches to employ in customizing the goals and meet the needs of the individual, and of appropriate providers to whom to refer individuals.

Application to Different Settings

The different settings in which the Strength-Based Approach could be used can be seen as expanding concentric circles (Figure 1). At the center is the use of this as a personal approach to consider our own careers as practitioners. In fact, that is a good test for the effectiveness of the approach.

Figure 1. Strength -Based Settings

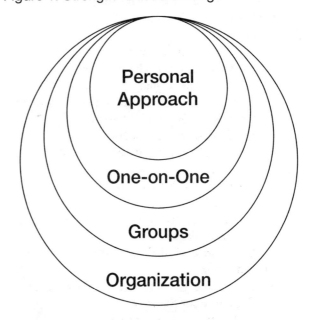

In the next circle, it could be used one-on-one with individuals, including clients, customers, students, or participants. If that is the intended use, it is important to be transparent about the approach and to educate the client about the intersection of career development and Appreciative Inquiry. It is also useful to work with individuals as they move through each phase of the model.

The third circle would include small groups or workshop settings. Transparency about the process is still important.

It is also possible, if the unit or organization is agile enough or small enough, to weave this approach throughout every action, policy, or process (which would be a fourth circle). If this were the intended use, it might be more from an Appreciative Inquiry perspective than a career development focus. The example of the women's shelter in Chapter I demonstrated how that might work. For larger organizations, it might be valuable to work with a qualified Appreciative Inquiry facilitator, so that the process is developed with an experienced consultant behind the scenes.

The Workshop Example

Applying the concepts of Appreciative Inquiry to career development is demonstrated in this example workshop. It is a two-session, six-hour workshop that has been delivered multiple times in a university environment. It has also served as the basis for numerous 60–90 minute presentations for practioners and educators. The following example provides slides, comments, and notes where needed.

A detailed agenda for this workshop is
I.   Introduction to the process
II. Discovery Phase
    a. The Appreciative Interview
        i.   Introduction to the Interview
        ii. Interview format
        iii. Interview partner and create summary
    b. Images of My Positive Future
        i. Guided imagery activity
        ii. Identify themes from the activity
III. Dream Phase
    a. Locating My Personal Themes
        i. Synthesize themes
        ii. Identify most exciting and engaging possibilities
    b. My Ideal Work-Life Scenario
IV. Design Phase
    a. Innovative Ways to Create My Future: My Sequence for Success
        i. Change, adapt, or adopt
        ii. Ten times more bold
    b. Sequence for Success: Shoulds, Wants, & Will
    c. Action Plan: My "WILL DO" Goal

    d. Cultivating My Sequence for Success
V.   Destiny Phase
    a. Possible Bumps in the Road to Building on My Strengths
    b. Sustaining My Positive Possibilities
VI. Valuing the Building on Your Strengths Process

There are two handouts for this workshop, the Building on Your Strengths Interview Guide (Appendix C), and the Building on Your Strengths Participant Guide (Appendix D). The presenter may choose to create additional handouts as needed. Typically, handouts of the PowerPoint presentation are provided so that the focus in the session is on listening and not on note taking. Occasionally participants will not want to write on the handouts so that they will have a "clean" copy. It might serve you well to have extra copies available so that the activity pace is not disrupted.

Basic informational slides are now provided followed by comments and related process notes.

Session One

Slide 1

> # Building on Your Strengths
>
> ---
>
> A Strength-Based Approach to Career Development

Slide 1 Comments: The Affirmative Topic choice is apparent in the title. "Building on Your Strengths" is chosen because it is empowering and eye-catching. As has been mentioned often, the language that is used matters and, in this case, sets the stage for what is ahead.

Below are additional helpful notes:

- This is a good time to ask people to briefly introduce themselves; interaction is key to the workshop.
- It is also wise (and ethical) to suggest that participants not make any important decisions during the workshop — such as leav-

ing a partner or quitting their jobs — without much more time and consideration.

- This is a good time to explore options not considered before.

Slides 2 and 3

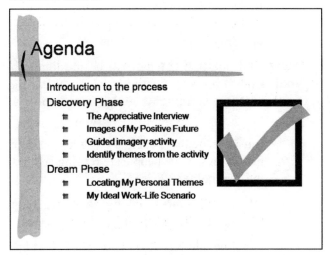

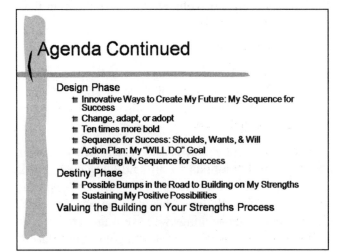

Slides 2 and 3 Comments: The agenda uses the Strength-Based Approach Cycle (modified from the Appreciative Inquiry 4-D Cycle). It works well to have participants introduce themselves, with the facilitator modeling an appropriate introduction. Typically the introductions are name, where they work, and interest in the workshop.

Following the individual introductions, it is useful to discuss the agenda and point to the unique nature of the activity, including:

- It is different than what they may have experienced in the past.
- It requires interaction and discussions with others.
- The learning is focused on the participant.

- Participants should pay attention to the language as the approach is introduced.

Slide 4

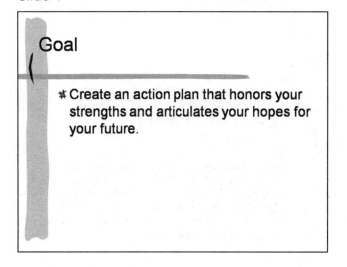

Slide 4 Comments: It is important to articulate the goal, encouraging participants to notice the language and purpose. The use of "your strengths" and "your hopes" is very intentional and demonstrates the focus on participants as individuals.

This is also a good time to explore with the participants what they are expecting from the experience.

One concern might be time. There is a careful balance in this workshop between helping set the stage by encouraging participation and interaction early on, and actually having enough time to complete the interview and participant guide. The first few times you do the workshop, it might be useful to be especially attentive to how much time is used in this first section.

Slide 5

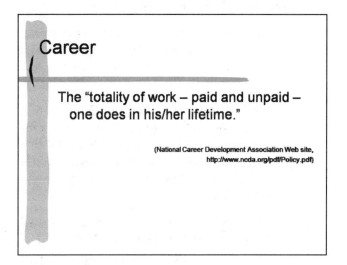

Slide 5 Comments: Before showing this slide, ask participants "How do you define career?" as a lead into the discussion about careers and career development. This tends to begin the process of discussing both paid and unpaid experiences and leads to the "in his/her lifetime" discussion.

Slide 6

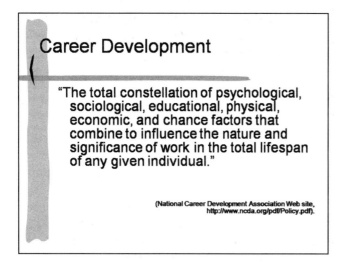

Slide 6 Comments: Two helpful lead questions to this slide are "What was the first thing you ever wanted to be?" and "What will be the final job in your life?" Process each of these questions separately.

The first question ("What was the first thing you ever wanted to be?") gets at the lifelong nature of career development. Many people discuss career development as beginning with their first job. However, the definition reframes career development much earlier, beginning with participant's thoughts as young children about their role in the world of work. Two follow up questions are: "And how old were you?", and "Where did that idea come from?" The learning points here are

- Career development begins long before our first jobs. It begins as young children begin to think about a place for themselves in the world

- These ideas come from everywhere — from family experience, from school, from jobs caretakers held, from feelings about different jobs, and from messages that society sends through television, radio, newspapers, and magazines.

- How we processed those messages created images for what we could or could not be.

- If there is a sense that gender played a part

in the participant's career development (i.e., girls should be nurses, boys should not), connecting with the participants on these stereotyped responses can open up productive conversations later in the workshop.

- If the expectations from parents and other family members played a part in the development of career aspirations.

The second question ("What will be the final job in your life?") moves participants to thinking about the future. Comments and learning points here are

- It used to be that people died about the time they retired. Now people are retiring and living for another 30 years.

- Often people are thinking about reaching their career dreams during this time period.

- Often people report taking care of children, siblings, or volunteering — something they are giving back.

- Others report creative endeavors like painting and writing.

- You might want to include the stimulus question, "What are you doing today to prepare for that future?"

The "big picture" processing goes back to career development definitions — all paid and unpaid work over the course of their lifetime, not just paid opportunities. Career development begins when we started to think about all those things we have wanted to be. Ask participants to consider the following questions during the workshop:

- What patterns or themes emerge over time related to experiences you have had?

- What patterns or themes emerge over time related to "What you have wanted to be?" or things in which you have an interest?

- Do these patterns or themes connect with your last job?

These questions can be inserted into the dialogue at any point and are useful as a transition to the next slide.

Slide 7

Integrative Life Planning

* Helps people see the "big picture" of their lives, their communities, and the larger society
* Six important principles:
  * it is a way of seeing the world that takes into account both personal development and the contexts within which we live;
  * a focus on valuing diversity and inclusivity;
  * it involves the examination of the relationship goals and achievement goals relative to society, the organization, the family, and the individual;
  * it explores connections and links between work and family;
  * it introduces spirituality, meaning, and purpose as key aspects of life planning; and
  * it emphasizes helping people manage change and understand their life choices, decisions, and transitions in a societal context (adapted from Hansen, 1997, pp. 11-18).

Slide 7 Comments: Integrative Life Planning is connected to the Strength-Based Approach through the "bigger picture" that connects us back to family, to the community, and to society. As you present this slide, highlight the six principles. These are, in part, the context within which you are developing.

Typically, relationships are highlighted along with spirituality, meaning, and purpose. Integrative Life Planning stimulates a review how we build important relationships in our lives, and asks us what relationships we want to have.

This is also about permission giving. The vital question is "How can I create, in the context of my life, a work-life scenario that fulfills me?" How does this then play into consideration as other career decisions are made? An example includes decisions related to competing demands between family and work. There is a "permission" component to this section that is the approval to weigh other important life variables — children, aging parents, good schools are examples — as heavily as career progression. Many people have never been told that it is OK, and is in fact healthy, to make work and life decisions together, on an equal basis.

Slide 8

Career Development Process

Comparing a Traditional Model and Appreciative Inquiry (the Strength-Based Approach)

Slide 8 Comments: This begins the introduction to the integration of career development and life planning.

Slide 9

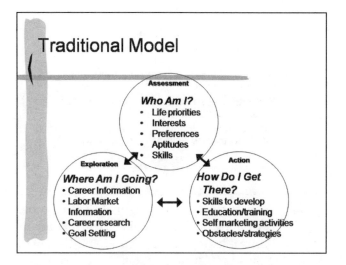

Slide 9 Comments: This model, discussed in detail in Chapter I, sets the stage for integration with Appreciative Inquiry. It is important to highlight the assessment, exploration, and action phases which are revised in the Strength-Based Approach.

Slide 10

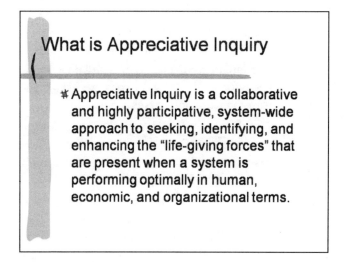

Slide 10 Comments: This introduces the idea of Appreciative Inquiry. It is important to highlight the "life-giving forces" since that is a foundation of the approach. The "performing optimally" is also important and is defined as a healthy work-life balance.

A possible prompt is to ask participants if they can identify what their "indicators" are when they are at their best. "When you are at your best, and things are going well and you think, 'I have a great life,' how do you know?"

Slide 11

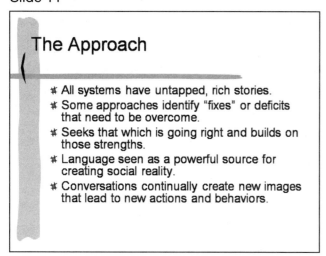

Slide 11 Comments: This begins to get into the importance of stories and story telling. Here it is important to talk about taking time to listen to others and to learn from the stories that others tell.

Areas to highlight include

- How do you come to understand the patterns over your lifespan?

- The discussion of "deficits" relates to how to best use energy and resources. "Are your resources better used moving yourself from something you are marginal at to average, or are your resources better used moving something you are good at to great?"

- The language we use matters and directs our behavior as do the questions we ask. Contrast the worst job versus the best job.

- Use the example of position descriptions or job announcements. Ask "How many of you read those and pick out the things you cannot do instead of all the things you can do?"

- "Where do you focus your listening?" The performance review example is a good one. In a feedback session, you might have 95% positive feedback, but all that is remembered after the session is the 5% of needed improvement or areas for growth. "Where would you rather focus?"

- "How much time and how many resources does it take for you to perpetuate yourself in something that creates unhappiness or that is not drawing on your strengths?"

- The discussion of new images is best presented through the women's shelter story.

Slide 12

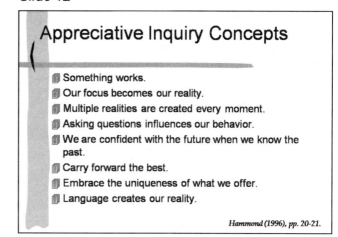

Slide 12 Comments: This is the heart of Appreciative Inquiry. Go slowly through each slide point. It would be good for you to understand how the pieces connect together since it is also at the center of the Strength-Based Approach. If you do not feel comfortable discussing Appreciative Inquiry, review Chapter II or utilize one of the resources listed at the end of this chapter.

Slide 13

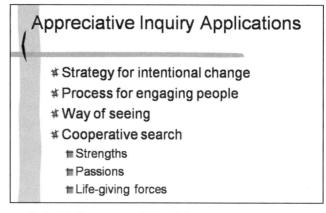

Slide 13 Comments: This slide gets at the action components behind Appreciative Inquiry.

Slide 14

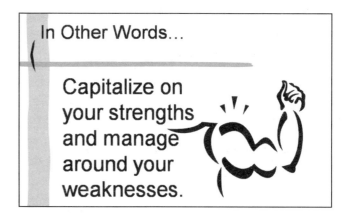

Slide 14 Comments: This originates from Buckingham and Clifton (2001) and provides a great opportunity to demonstrate that research from other fields validates this approach:

- This slide is based on Buckingham and Coffman's (1999) survey using meta-analysis of data from a 1998 survey of over 105,000 employees from over 2,500 business units, which was combined with data from in-depth interviews with over 80,000 managers in 400 companies and led to Buckingham & Clifton's (2001) "strength revolution at work."
- It also links to strengths-based findings from the Signature Strength research and research on Positive Psychology (see Chapter I).

Slides 15 and 16

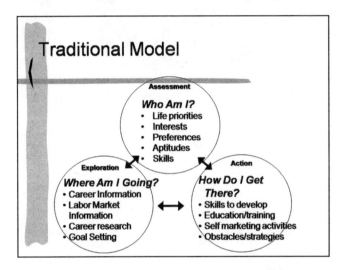

The Strength-Based Approach

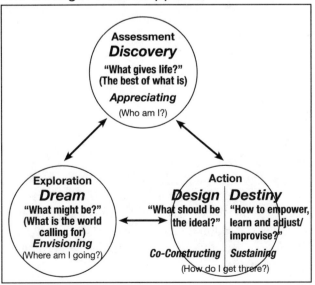

Slides 15 and 16 Comments: This highlights the transition and blending of Appreciative Inquiry with career development which leads to the Strength-Based Approach. It is important to help participants note that the assessment, exploration, and action are still embedded, although the appreciative language changes the words to appreciating, envisioning, co-constructing, and sustaining.

It is helpful to toggle between the two slides as you talk so participants can see the language change (rather than go from memory).

Slide 17

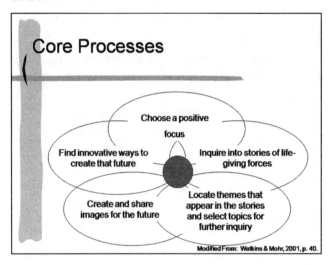

Slide 17 Comments: These five core underlying processes direct the Strength-Based Approach. It is helpful to walk through each process and provide some example or a brief look ahead to how each will be experienced in the workshop.

Slide 18

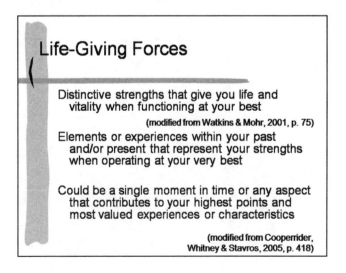

Slide 18 Comments: The notion of 'life-giving forces" is sometimes difficult to grasp but is usually clarified quite easily through illustration. It is helpful to provide an example for participants. One example might be "when I am working on creating Web sites, I lose track of time and am so engaged that time passes much faster than I realize."

Slide 19

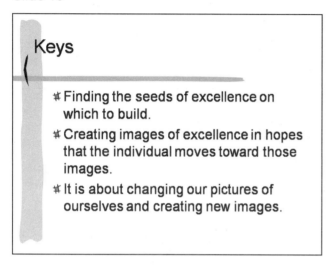

Keys

* Finding the seeds of excellence on which to build.
* Creating images of excellence in hopes that the individual moves toward those images.
* It is about changing our pictures of ourselves and creating new images.

Slide 19 Comments: This provides a short summary of the process ahead. This brings closure, for the most part, to the introductory presentation. The emphasis during the rest of the workshop becomes more experiential and interactive using the "Building on Your Strengths Participant Guide."

After Slide 19, it is usually a good time for a break. When the group reconvenes, begin with Slide 20. A good question to restart the workshop is "Who can summarize the key points of what we have talked about so far?" It usually is a nice way to re-engage the group.

Slide 20

Building on Your Strengths

Introduction

* Please read each question, or say it in your own words and then allow time for the interviewee to reflect and answer.
* Encourage your interviewee to talk.
* Enjoy the experience.
* Take notes as you go.
* When the interview is complete, share with your interviewee what you learned that most interested you and thank the person for her or his time.
* Please be sure to give the interviewee her or his *Interview Guide* and the *Interview Summary Sheet* that you completed.

Slide 20 Comments: Participants have been redirected to the "Building on Your Strengths Interview Guide" at this point (which is described in detail in Appendix C).

It is a good idea to go through each point on this Introductory slide slowly and articulate each instruction, connecting it back to the positive core and the appreciative approach. For more information on the actual activity, see Appendix B. It is important to leave at least 40–45 for each interview (or 90 minutes for the interviews and the summary).

Once participants have interviewed each other, completed the summary sheet, and shared that with their partner, it will be near the time to end the first session.

It is helpful to process all the interviews with participants at the end of the interview and summary session. Possible prompts include

- Any reactions or responses to the interviews?
- Any surprises?
- How did the interviews connect with the concepts discussed at the beginning?
- Any reactions or responses to the summary feedback about themes and patterns from your interviewer?
- Let's summarize the most important points from this session...

This ends Session One.

Session Two

Begin by asking participants:

- What do you remember from last time?
- What were the key concepts?
- How do the interviews play into the experience?
- What struck you most about your first experience?

Once you have begun the conversation, decide which slides you need to use to familiarize participants with the concepts and model. Once that reconnecting process has occurred, move into the next activity.

Slides 21 through 25

Slides 21 through 25 Comments: The first slide reintroduces the overall process.

Slide 22 moves the workshop back into the "Building on Your Strengths Participant Guide." Slides 23 through 25 serve as introductions to the activities. All the activities are described in detail in Appendix B. In addition, the handouts for these activities are in the Participant Guide (Appendix D.).

Process

* Look at experiences and times when things are going well – times when you felt excited and successful.
* Create an image of what you want.
* Understand how others work with successful situations.
* Create a common image that can be continually regenerated.

Locating My Personal Themes

* Review and complete the *Locating My Personal Themes* sheet.
* Reconnect with your dialogue partner to discuss the themes you have identified.

Creating Ideal Work-Life Scenario

* Best work situation?
* Most important to carry forward?
* **My ideal work-life scenario…**
  * Present tense
  * Positive
  * Energizing language
  * Bold & provocative
* Give energy and feeling of purpose.

Innovative Ways: My Sequence of Success

* What could you change, adapt or adopt to get to the ideal work-life scenario?
* If you were to be 10X more bold, what would you do?

Sequence of Success

* Shoulds, Wants, & Will (p. 9)
* Action Plan (pp. 10-11)
  * Description on pp. 12-13
* Possible Bumps in the Road
  * Ignore
  * Respond – alone or with support from others
  * Respond later – alone or with support from others
* Sustaining & Valuing (p. 14)

Slide 26

Goals

* Create an action plan that honors your strengths and articulates your hopes for your future.
* See your life and the world through a positive, life-enhancing lens.

Slide 26 Comments: This slide is the first step in closure. It revisits the goal and adds an additional goal (a wish for the future perhaps). It also might be a good time to revisit the definition of Appreciative Inquiry and how it connects to career development;

Some possible points to include:

* This process is about choosing the positive as a focus of the inquiry, and looking at life-giving forces and what gives energy.
* It is also about distinctive strengths that show you when you are operating at your best.
* It is what makes you passionate and connects to those themes and images of work-life balance, and to finding innovative ways to get to that future.
* The process begins by choosing the positive as the focus of energy and looking for those keys, or seeds of excellence, on which to build.

Slides 27 and 28

Appreciative Inquiry Resources

* Annis Hammond, S. (1996). *The thin book of Appreciative Inquiry*. Plano, TX: Kodiak Consulting.
* Buckingham, M., & Clifton, D. O. (2001). *Now, Discover Your Strengths*. NY: The Free Press.
* Cooperrider, D. L., Whitney, D., and Stavros, J. M. (2005). *Appreciative Inquiry Handbook: The First in a Series of AI Workbooks for Leaders of Change*. Brunswick, OH: Crown Custom Publishing, Inc., & San Francisco: Berrett-Koehler Publishers, Inc. Cooperrider, D., Sorenson, P. F., Whitney, D., & Yaeger, T. F. (1999). *Appreciative Inquiry: Rethinking human organization toward a positive theory of change*. Champaign, IL: Stipes Publishing L.L.C.
* Magruder Watkins, J. & Mohr, B. (2001). *Appreciate Inquiry: Change at the Speed of Imagination*. San Francisco: Jossey-Bass Publishers, Inc.
* Hansen, L. S. (1997). *Integrative Life Planning : Critical Tasks for Career Development and Changing Life Patterns*. San Francisco: Jossey-Bass Publishers, Inc.
* Whitney, D., Cooperrider, D., Trosten-Bloom, A., & Kaplin, B. S. (2002). *Encyclopedia of positive questions: Volume one: Using Appreciative Inquiry to bring out the best in your organization*. Euclid, OH: Lakeshore Communications.

Online AI Opportunities

* Appreciative Inquiry Commons
  http://appreciativeinquiry.cwru.edu/
* What is Appreciative Inquiry?
  http://www.thinbook.com/lib/thinbook/whatisai.pdf
* Appreciative Inquiry: An Overview
  http://www.cditrainers.org/appreciative_inquiry-overview.htm

Slides 27 and 28 Comments: Point out that just as individual careers are a process, so is learning about career development, Appreciative Inquiry, and the Strength-Based Approach. The Appreciative Inquiry Commons is one of the best resources available online, particularly since it is usually kept up to date.

Slide 29

Valuing the Process

* Please complete the "Valuing the Building on Your Strengths Process" sheet
* There are copies of the entire packet and the interview guide if you are interested

Slide 29 Comments: This is a reinforcing shift away from evaluation to a valuing process which, in terms of language, connects to the positive. The questions are also stated with an appreciative approach. This feedback can be used in several different ways: it can be the sheet that is used to process the experience from the individual's perspective; it can be used to provide feedback about the experience for the facilitator; or it can be used as both an individual processing activity that is then used for course feedback.

It is a good idea to have additional packets for people if they are interested in getting a "clean copy" to share with others.

Slide 30

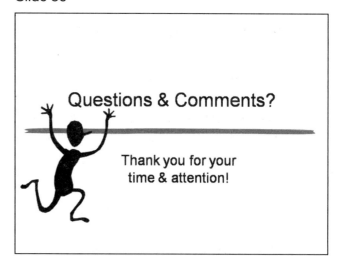

Slide 30 Comments: It is always a good idea to leave some time for comments. This is also the place where the facilitator can provide referral sources for those participants who would like a follow-up appointment.

Resources

Here are a number of useful print resources and a short description of each.

* Hammond, S. A. (1996). *The thin book of Appreciative Inquiry.* Plano, TX: Kodiak Consulting.

  This book is a great primer and an overview on the basics of Appreciative Inquiry. The format is easy to read with interesting stories used to depict the ideas presented. (63 pages)

* Cooperrider, D. L., Whitney, D., & Stavros, J. M. (2005). *Appreciative Inquiry handbook: The first in a series of AI workbooks for leaders of change.* Brunswick, OH: Crown

Custom Publishing, Inc., & San Francisco: Berrett-Koehler Publishers, Inc.

The premier book on Appreciative Inquiry. It includes background, history, learning applications, PowerPoint presentations, and selected "classic" Appreciative Inquiry articles. It is described as the "ultimate guide to Appreciative Inquiry" for good reason. (430 pages)

- Hansen, L. S. (1997). *Integrative Life Planning: Critical tasks for career development and changing life patterns.* San Francisco: Jossey-Bass Publishers, Inc.

A useful book that, when it was published, was seen as a new way of thinking about career development. It weaves together family, community, meaningful work, pluralism, spirituality, and life purpose as critical factors in life planning. (358 pages)

- Preskill, H., & Coghlan, A. T. (eds). (Winter 2003). *New Directions for Evaluation, no. 100: Using Appreciative Inquiry in evaluation.* San Francisco: Wiley Periodicals, Inc.

An excellent resource for evaluating the Appreciative Inquiry approach across a variety of contexts and with different populations. (103 pages)

- Watkins, J. M., & Mohr, B. J. (2001). *Appreciative Inquiry: Change at the speed of imagination.* San Francisco: Jossey-Bass/Pfeiffer.

Each chapter is very detailed and often has at least one case study to demonstrate the concepts. This book also has an excellent history of Appreciative Inquiry, as well as helpful meeting agendas and other supporting materials. (241 pages)

- Whitney, D., Cooperrider, D., Trosten-Bloom, A., & Kaplin, B. S. (2002). *Encyclopedia of positive questions: Volume one: Using Appreciative Inquiry to bring out the best in your organization.* Euclid, OH: Lakeshore Communications.

Positive questions in over 40 areas along with sample appreciative interview guides and a "how to" chapter. It is very useful when creating an Appreciative Inquiry interview guide or planning an event where an appreciative approach is going to be used. (146 pages)

Here are some online resources that may also be helpful.

- Appreciative Inquiry Commons
http://appreciativeinquiry.cwru.edu/

One of the most helpful and up-to-date educational Web sites available. From introductory information to networking opportunities to research, this site has everything needed to better understand Appreciative Inquiry and connect with like-minded learners.

- Appreciative Inquiry: An Overview
http://www.cditrainers.org/appreciative_inquiry-overview.htm

A brief yet comprehensive overview of appreciative Inquiry concepts and constructs.

Conclusion

The Strength-Based Approach to career development is based on the simple assumptions that every individual has something that works well and that these strengths can be the starting point for creating positive change. Inviting individuals to participate in dialogues and share stories about their past and present achievements, assets, unexplored potentials, innovations, strengths, elevated thoughts, opportunities, benchmarks, high-point moments, lived values, traditions, core and distinctive competencies, expressions of wisdom, insights into the deeper personal spirit and soul, and visions of valued and possible futures can identify a "positive change core." From this, the Strength-Based Approach to career development links the energy of the positive core directly to any change agenda. This link creates energy and excitement and a desire to move toward a personal dream (adapted from Appreciative Inquiry description found in Cooperrider, Whitney, & Stavros, 2005, p. 3).

The Strength-Based Approach is more than a tool; it is a way of seeing the world that is positive and focuses on building upon strengths rather than on fixing or repairing deficits. It suggests that the questions we ask drive the direction and focus of our actions and behavior. The primary technique used in this approach is an appreciative interview, from which the rest of the process unfolds. The Strength-Based Approach is not a new theory of career development; it can be integrated into many different theoretical perspectives.

The reframing of career development interventions using the Strength-Based Approach offers individuals an energizing way to assess, explore, and plan for a more positive work-life balance. If the goal is to create an action plan that honors an individual's strengths and articulates her or his hopes for the future, the Strength-Based Approach provides a process for reaching that goal.

Appendices

Appendix A:
Transition from
Career Development
to the Strength-Based Approach

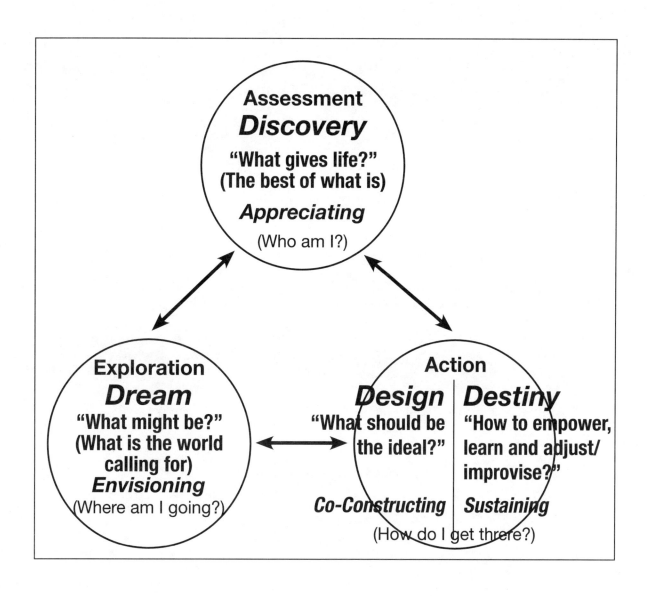

Assessment
Discovery

"What gives life?"
(The best of what is)

Appreciating

(Who am I?)

Exploration
Dream

"What might be?"
(What is the world
calling for)
Envisioning

(Where am I going?)

Action
Design

"What should be
the ideal?"

Co-Constructing

Destiny

"How to empower,
learn and adjust/
improvise?"

Sustaining

(How do I get there?)

Appendix B:
Activities

Activity 1: Building on Your Strengths *Interview Guide*

Purpose

To guide the interviewer through an appreciative interview and to capture the information provided by the interviewee

Learning Objectives

- To uncover the best of "what is" in the interviewee's life experiences
- To practice viewing personal experiences from a positive perspective
- To identify strengths and positive patterns or themes in the interviewee's life

Rationale

This activity is a foundation for the Building on Your Strengths process. It is based on the Strength-Based Approach to career development and is the initial data gathering activity.

Setting

One-on-one, classroom or workshop setting

Time Required

100 minutes

Materials

The Building on Your Strengths *Interview Guide*

Instructions

1. Direct participants to the *Interview Guide*
2. Ask participants to find a partner (there can be a group of three if needed; if so, adjust the timing for that group) and to briefly introduce themselves if they do not know the other person.
3. Introduce the Strength-Based Approach
   "Before you begin, it is important to understand what you are going to be doing as it may be a little different from what you have done in the past. This Participant Guide is intended to pilot you through an appreciative interview process.

   You will be asked questions about times when you saw things working at their best in your work and your life. Many times the focus of the questions in life is on those things that are not working well, or the problems you are experiencing, so that you can find the best solution to "fixing" the challenge. This experience is intended to be different; you are asked to try to learn about things at their best — the successes — so that you can find out what works and find ways to infuse more of the positive core into your life and work. This journey encourages both the acceptance of a positive perspective as a world view (in contrast to a deficit-based view), and the development of language that supports a more positive process for exploring your career development needs.

   The purpose of this process is to create a positive self-image and allow you to envision even greater possibilities based on your strengths. The process will also help you to connect your work and life decisions to others around you who serve as life partners and support networks. The end result of the interview will help you better understand the "life-giving" forces that provide vitality and distinctive competence to your life and work.

As a part of this process, you will look at

- The core factors that enable your success
- Your story as it is being written, unfolding in the presence of a dialogue partner through the interview process
- The learning you gain from your experience when you examine closely those moments when you have been at your best

- Your most effective practices, strengths, and best qualities that are necessary for you to preserve as you make other changes in your life

- How your positive past — the best of your experiences — can help you be more daring and innovative as you think about your true potential

- The future that you envision for yourself including your hopes and positive images

- Building a life through positive and intentional planning that integrates the best of who you are with those with whom you share your life."

4. Explain the process. They will have approximately 40 minutes to interview each other using the Guide for at least the starter questions. They are invited to use additional questions that pertain to the topic. There is no need to hurry through the interview. After they have interviewed each other, they should complete the summary sheet and share the responses with their partner. After the summary sheet has been discussed, the participants will give it to the person they interviewed.

5. Introduce the Interview Activity

"The purpose of the interview is appreciating the interviewee's strengths and exploring what "gives life" and energy to the interviewee. The process is focused on the interviewee initially, and you, the interviewer, will get to share your focused listening later in the process.

- Please read each question, or say it in your own words, and then allow time for the interviewee to reflect and answer. Silence is okay, so please do not feel like you need to fill the empty space. If needed, repeat the question if that seems like it might help.

- Encourage your interviewee to talk. Listen with curiosity and wonder. Nonverbal encouragers like gently nodding your head, taking notes, and demonstrating an active listening posture (facing the interviewee directly, occasionally leaning forward, keeping a comfortable distance between you and the interviewee, and being attentive). Verbal encouragers or prompting such as paraphrasing and asking probing follow-up questions is also useful.

- Enjoy the experience of learning about someone else and how that person does what she or he does. Smile and remember the more at ease you are, the more at ease the interviewee will be.

- Make notes as you go and then record key points on the Building on Your Strengths Interview Summary Sheet that follows the interview questions.

- When the interview is complete, share with your interviewee what you learned that most interested you and thank the person for her or his time.

- Please be sure to give the interviewee her or his Interview Guide and the Interview Summary Sheet that you completed. This is important since the story the interviewee shared was her or his personal story and she or he is the owner of the product."

6. Ask participants to begin and tell participants that you will check their progress in 30 minutes. This is done so that the facilitator can manage the group time. After 30 minutes, check their progress. They should be at least up to the second question in the first interview. Ideally, they should be ready to move into the third question or have already moved there. Continue to check progress until approximately 80 minutes has passed. Be sure that they also complete the summary sheet for the interview.

7. Process the experience

- "What are your reactions and thoughts related to the interviews?"

- "Did anyone find it difficult to stay focused on positive images and experiences?"

- "How would this have been different if the focus had been on the worst experiences of your life?"

- "Any reactions or surprises when you heard the summary?"

- "How well did this capture, for you, the best of 'what is'?"

8. Explain that this is one set of "data" they can use for building their action plan and that there are other ways to also generate ideas about how to build on their strengths.

9. Ask participants to be sure to return the *Interview Guide* to the person who was interviewed.

Discussion

If you have more time, the interview is a great place to allow extra time. One alternative is to have participants get as far as possible and meet with their partner between sessions or, if this is part of a half- or full-day workshop, blend this activity into a break allowing a little extra time.

Assessment

The effectiveness of this activity is assessed by the beginning articulation, for participants, of what the best of "what is" includes.

Activity 2: Images of My Positive Future

Purpose

To guide participants through a life-work guided imagery activity which allows participants to be more creative, connect images of their life as they look ahead, and consider what they feel they have been "called" to do.

Learning Objectives

To seek out and preserve that which the interviewees do best, those characteristics of which they are most proud, and characteristics that create success and that they wish to build into your future

Rationale

To stimulate new images and ideas, it is useful to use a variety of techniques such as guided imagery.

Setting

One-on-one, classroom or workshop setting

Time Required

30 minutes

Materials

The "Images of My Positive Future" activity found in the Building on Your Strengths Participant Guide

Instructions

1. Direct participants to the "Images of My Positive Future" activity found in the Building on Your Strengths Participant Guide

2. Explain the process.

   • They will be participating in a guided imagery activity that is intended to encourage participants to think creatively about their future.

   • The activity allows participants to let go of the things that currently are of concern to them, and asks participants to think freely about the ideal future for themselves.

   • For many people, this type of activity is very helpful as it allows participants to develop a picture or image of the future

   • If they are not comfortable with guided imagery activities, they are welcome to sit back quietly and relax until the activity is complete.

   • Following the activity, they will be asked to process their response using the worksheet.

   • "Any questions about the process? [pause] Then let's begin."

3. Read the guided imagery script slowly with pauses at the end of sentences. Note: This script is intended to have the participants think about a time three years from today.

   "Please get comfortable, close your eyes if you like; think about the themes and patterns you have identified. Take a deep breath in, feel it fill your lungs. Now exhale slowly and feel your body begin to relax. Again, take a deep breath and let it out slowly as your thoughts keep replaying the themes and patterns.

   Imagine those themes have been implemented fully in your everyday life and work. Imagine that those life experiences from the past are now the typical, everyday experiences in your life. Your life is full of images, feelings, and conversations representing those positive themes and patterns.

   We are now going to travel ahead to your future. Put yourself three years ahead into the future. Imagine that your day is just beginning and you are preparing for work. You are energized and eager to begin your day because you know you will be spending your day doing work that draws on your strengths and provides you with great satisfaction. As you look around, you see the world just as you hoped it would be. What do you see? Picture in your mind what is happening.

   Who is around you? How is the world different? As you imagine your day ahead, what pictures emerge that continue to provide you with energy and enthusiasm. How does it feel to see those pictures?

You begin to reflect back to the journey you have been on over the past three years. How did this come about? What helped it to happen? What are the things that supported this journey? Who did you draw on for support in your success? What makes this vision so compelling to you?

Consider how quickly you got to where you are. How were you able to realize this vision with such unsurpassed speed? As you remember your progress, you feel good about creating such a healthy and meaningful change in your work and in your life.

We are now going to return to today — this place, this time. Open your eyes and return to this room at your own speed. When ready, jot down a few words in your interview guide that describe your experience."

4. Allow participants time to rejoin you at their own pace. Reinforce that they should respond to the three questions on the worksheet.

5. Once they have completed the worksheet, ask participants to find a partner and briefly share what they saw, heard, or felt.

6. Process the activity by asking

   • "Were you able to get a sense for what life would be like for you in the future?"

   • "Were you able to connect to any peak experiences? How did that feel?"

7. Thank participants for participating in the activity.

Discussion

There are some people who are not comfortable with guided imagery and it is important not to force participants into participating. It is also the case, at times, that participants who might be reluctant at first may actually participate if given "permission" to sit out.

Assessment

The effectiveness of this activity is assessed by the degree to which participants are beginning to articulate the images they have of their future.

Activity 3: Locating My Personal Themes

Purpose

To synthesize any earlier activities that provided opportunities to identify themes or patterns.

Learning Objectives

- To identify their strengths
- To begin to articulate their hopes for the future

Rationale

It is important to synthesize many different sets of information as a way to begin to articulate the picture of who they are.

Setting

One-on-one, classroom or workshop setting

Time Required

30 minutes

Materials

The "Locating My Personal Themes" activity found in the Building on Your Strengths Participant Guide

Instructions

1. Direct participants to the "Locating My Personal Themes" activity found in the Building on Your Strengths Participant Guide

2. Explain the process.
   - "Look back over the activities where you have discovered or been reminded about the important themes in your life."
   - "Use the worksheet to guide you in reflecting on those themes and what led to the development of those themes."
   - Once they have completed the sheets, they will be asked to find a partner.
   - "Any questions about the process? [pause] Then let's look at the introduction to the activity."

3. Ask participants to "Please take a few moments to consider the themes, patterns or areas that appeared in the stories and in your dialogue with your partner and in the image of your positive future. Please identify the themes and patterns and list them here."

4. Provide an example demonstrating the process by creating a short scenario. Pretend that one partner shared three childhood experiences: having a paper route, selling ice cream from an ice cream bicycle cart they bought from a neighbor, and the enjoyment felt from a successful lemonade stand. The pattern from these three experiences is "always looking for an entrepreneurial opportunity."

5. Upon completion individually, ask participants to find a partner and share their responses.

6. Process briefly as a group.

Assessment

The effectiveness of this activity is assessed by the degree to which participants can begin to articulate patters or themes in their lives.

Activity 4: My Ideal Work-Life Scenario

Purpose
To articulate the participant's work-life scenario.

Learning Objectives
- To create a work-life scenario from positive experiences carrying forward the best of the past.
- To connect the experience to personal source of energy and purpose.

Rationale
Understanding the direction and the goal in planning helps to effectively create behaviors consistent in moving toward that goal.

Setting
One-on-one, classroom or workshop setting

Time Required
40 minutes

Materials
The "My Ideal Work-Life Scenario" activity found in the Building on Your Strengths Participant Guide

Instructions
1. Direct participants to the "My Ideal Work-Life Scenario" activity found in the Building on Your Strengths Participant Guide
2. Ask participants to complete the statements and answer the question. This is intended to be an ideal. Encourage participants to include connections to family, important relationships, and other factors that help participants feel "balanced" in their lives and work.
3. Remind participants to write their statement in the present tense, and to be sure it is positive, uses energizing language, and is bold and provocative.
4. Once completed, ask participants to find a partner with whom they will share their scenario and the ways it gives them energy and a sense of purpose.
5. Process briefly as a group.

Discussion
Occasionally it is difficult to think about the "ideal" without adding possible barriers or obstacles. It is important to help the participant to stay focused on positive and energizing images and feelings that lead to this ideal scenario.

Assessment
The effectiveness of this activity is assessed by the degree to which participants develop their ideal work-life scenario.

Activity 5: Innovative Ways to Create the Future: My Sequence for Success

Purpose

To begin moving toward the ideal work-life scenario developed in Activity 4.

Learning Objectives

- To identify current resources that could be directed or redirected toward achieving their ideal work-life scenario
- To think more boldly about possible strategies for success toward their goals.

Rationale

This very purposefully engages the participant in thinking about how to organize or prioritize existing resources toward their goals while at the same time encouraging participants to think "out of the box" about creative ways that they could also be successful.

Setting

One-on-one, classroom or workshop setting

Time Required

30 minutes

Materials

The "Innovative Ways to Create the Future: My Sequence for Success" activity found in the Building on Your Strengths Participant Guide. Note: Must have completed the "My Ideal Work-Life Scenario."

Instructions

1. Direct participants to the "Innovative Ways to Create the Future: My Sequence for Success" activity found in the Building on Your Strengths Participant Guide.
2. Have participants review and respond to these two questions:
   a. "What could you change, adapt, or adopt in your current situation to get the sense of purpose and energy gained through your ideal position?"
   b. "If you were to be TEN TIMES MORE BOLD in the pursuit of your ideal work-life scenario, what would you do?"
3. Once completed, ask participants to find a partner with whom they will share their responses.
4. Process briefly as a group.

Assessment

The effectiveness of this activity is assessed by the degree to which participants can begin to think creatively about how they use their time and resources.

Activity 6: Sequence for Success: Shoulds, Wants, & Will

Purpose

To identify one or two priorities on which the action plan is built.

Learning Objectives

- To understand their personal decision-making processes
- To motivate participants to begin taking action

Rationale

It is very easy to get through the planning phase and never actually take action or change behaviors. This activity helps participants focus on a beginning step with which they can start.

Setting

One-on-one, classroom or workshop setting

Time Required

15 minutes

Materials

The "Sequence for Success: Shoulds, Wants, & Will" activity found in the Building on Your Strengths Participant Guide.

Instructions

1. Direct participants to the "Sequence for Success: Shoulds, Wants, & Will" activity found in the Building on Your Strengths Participant Guide

2. Ask the participant to

   a. Identify five things they feel that they should do in terms of their career and career development.

   b. Once that is complete, ask participants to choose from the list of five "shoulds," three things that they actually "want" to do. Ask participants to rewrite those three in the new spaces on the bottom half of the worksheet, one for each dashed line. Also ask participants to consider how each "want" connects with their strengths.

   c. Choose one item from the "wants" list as something they actually "will" do. This serves as the starting point for their action planning.

3. Process briefly as a group.

Assessment

Participants have one clear "will" from which they will build a work-life scenario.

Activity 7: Action Plan: My "WILL DO" Goal

Purpose
To create an action plan and strategies . . .

Learning Objectives
- To learn the process of action planning
- To better understand what is important to participants as they develop personal career action plan

Rationale
The work begins with a plan. Built into the plan are components to evaluate the plan as it being developed, as well as opportunities to identify strategies and support structures.

Setting
One-on-one, classroom or workshop setting

Time Required
45 minutes

Materials
The "Action Plan: My 'WILL DO' Goal" activity found in the Building on Your Strengths Participant Guide.

Instructions
1. Direct participants to the "Action Plan: My 'WILL DO' Goal" activity found in the Building on Your Strengths Participant Guide including the "Cultivating My Sequence for Success."
2. Have participants quietly read "Cultivating My Sequence for Success" and highlight key points.
3. Work with participants to develop their action plan.
   a. The "I will" statement demonstrates commitment and should be followed by a positively-stated goal. An example of a positively-stated goal for someone who wants to quit smoking might be "I will have healthier lungs in six months." A non-positively-stated goal for the same person might be "I will give up smoking in the next six months." There are two main differences between these goals:
      i. the focus in the first is on what the person has to gain rather than what the person has to give up
      ii. the first statement creates an image of healthy lungs versus the image of lungs damaged by smoking.

   In the Strength-Based Approach, the hope would be that the goals are positively stated and connected to images that are energizing and exciting.

   b. The beginning date should be as soon as possible and the completion date should be within a reasonable time period so that motivation is not lost.
   c. The four brief questions should all be responded to with a "yes:"
      i. Yes-able? Refers to the question, "Am I likely to get support from the important actors in my life" for this goal?"
      ii. "Does this reflect my ideal?" (Connects back to the Ideal Work-Life Scenario.)
      iii. "Is this driven by my strengths? Does this connect to carrying my best forward (as it should)?
      iv. "Is it my influence? Is this something that I can act on? Is it within my control or ability to affect or change?"
   d. The "To Do" list are the steps necessary to achieve the goal. Once the steps are written in, the blanks to the right of the steps are used to sequence the steps. The steps can be sequenced in order of importance or in the actual progression in which they will occur. A final step is to review the steps to see if there is one step that would have the greatest impact.

4. Once completed, ask participants to find a partner with whom they can share their responses.

5. The final discussion on this activity includes the following learning points:

    a. "Goals are more effective if you tell someone.

    b. Goals are more effective if you write them down and put them somewhere you will see them often.

    c. Goals are achieved when connected back to something important, like work-life balance, or happiness."

Discussion

It is intended that only one goal be worked on at a time. There is an additional sheet in the packet so that once the first goal is complete, participants can begin working on a second goal.

Assessment

Participants have an articulated goal based on their hopes for their future.

Activity 8: Possible Bumps in the Road to Building on My Strengths

Purpose

To identify potential challenges or "bumps" that might inhibit the successful completion of the goal.

Learning Objectives

- To project possible inhibitors to successful completion of the goal
- To feel like it is possible to ignore or respond to the possible inhibitors at a later time

Rationale

Identifying challenges is always difficult and takes energy away from any planning process. Many plans end at this point, and all the time, effort, and creativity is lost. The purpose in this activity is to model good planning (by identifying the challenges) and effective responding techniques (by responding, responding later, and ignoring).

Setting

One-on-one, classroom or workshop setting

Time Required

25 minutes

Materials

The "Possible Bumps in the Road to Building on My Success" activity found in the Building on Your Strengths Participant Guide.

Instructions

1. Direct participants to the "Possible Bumps in the Road to Building on My Success" activity found in the Building on Your Strengths Participant Guide
2. Ask the participant to
   a. Identify any items that might take energy away from them successfully achieving their goal, including any areas where they might need to "manage their weaknesses."
   b. Choose the bumps that are within their ability to influence.
   c. elect their desired action, which could be
      i. Ignoring the obstacle,
      ii. Choosing to deal with the obstacle later, or
      iii. Decide to respond to the obstacle.
   d. If participants decide to respond, decide who, within the important actors in their lives, can assist them in dealing with this obstacle.
   e. Remind participants to be sure to include additional action steps in their Sequence for Success to deal with these bumps.
3. Find a partner and brainstorm additional possibilities for working with these bumps.
4. Process briefly as a group. Reminding participants to work on those items within their influence, focus on their strengths, and focus on the positive images for their future.

Assessment

Participants have identified and prioritized the importance of the challenges to their plan and have decided which action to take.

Appendix C:
Building on Your Strengths
Interview Guide

Building on Your Strengths
Interview Guide

Interviewee:_____

Interviewer:_____ Date:_____

Questions

1. Let's begin by talking about a time when you felt most happy in your career —— a time when you were having fun and doing a great job. Describe the situation. Explore these areas with your partner.

   a. What was it that created a sense of happiness and fulfillment?

   b. Who was involved? What did the person(s) do?

   c. What did you do that contributed to your own sense of happiness and fulfillment?

   d. As you think about that time when you felt most happy, what workplace characteristics stand out for you as important or necessary for your happiness and success?

   e. What about that time made it meaningful?

Notes:

2. There are often times in our lives when we feel particularly energized and positive. Looking at all your life experiences, can you recall a peak work or learning experience when you felt most alive, most involved, or most excited about your work? Possible areas to look at include

   a. What made it an exciting experience?

   b. Who were the significant others in the experience?

   c. Why were they significant?

   d. What was it about you that made it a peak experience?

   e. What were the most important factors in the work that helped to make it a peak experience? (Please explore this to better understand. Examples might be relationships, leadership, resources, etc.)

Notes:

3. Let's talk for a moment about the things that you value deeply — specifically, the aspects you value about yourself, the nature of your work, and the work environment.

   a. Without being humble, what do you value the most about yourself as a human being, a friend, a parent, a citizen, or a son/daughter?

   b. When you are feeling best about your work, what do you value about the task itself?

   c. What about the workplace do you value most?

   d. What is the single most important thing that your work has contributed to your life?

Notes:

4. If you had three wishes for your career, what would they be? Please list three things in order of priority.

Wish One:

Wish Two:

Wish Three:

Thank you for sharing your stories with me. Now, I would like to take a minute to collect my thoughts so that I can share with you some of the themes and patterns that, from my perspective, seemed to emerge as we were talking.

Summary Sheet

[Please Note: This is completed by the interviewer for the interviewee]

Please complete this summary sheet following your interview. Reflect on what you heard and make note of the themes, patterns, stories, and quotes you heard. You are, in a sense, mining for the life-giving forces that come through in the interview. The theme is the "idea or concept about what is present in the stories that people report are the times of greatest excitement, creativity, and reward." For example, during the interview you might hear "a feeling of success" or "clarity about purpose" or "fun and excitement." These phrases are 'themes'" (Watkins & Mohr, 2001, p. 119).

The goal of the summary sheet is to share the themes and patterns that came through in the interview, and to capture the moment on paper. Ultimately, each interviewee controls how the information impacts her or his decision making and career development.

1. What did you hear the person describing in the interview as her or his life-giving forces?

2. Identify three to five major themes or patterns that emerged from the interview?

3. What were the most quotable quotes that came from your conversation?

4. Please summarize what you heard, felt, or saw as the interviewee's strengths.

Interviewer:_____ Date:_____

Appendix D:
Building on Your Strengths
Participant Guide

Building on Your Strengths
Participant Guide

Created By:

Don Schutt, Ph.D., NCC, LPC, MCDP

189 Bascom Hall

500 Lincoln Drive

Madison, WI 53706

dschutt@ohr.wisc.edu

608-263-1016

Important note: This Interview Guide has two primary sources that were extensively drawn upon in developing the following materials: Cooperrider, D. L., Whitney, D., and Stavros, J. M. (2005). *Appreciative Inquiry Handbook: The First in a Series of AI Workbooks for Leaders of Change.* Brunswick, OH: Crown Custom Publishing, Inc., & San Francisco: Berrett-Koehler Publishers, Inc.; and Watkins, J. M. and Mohr, B. J. (2001). *Appreciative Inquiry: Change at the Speed of Imagination.* San Francisco: Jossey-Bass/Pfeiffer. In addition, conceptually the Guide also draws on the work in Hansen, L. S. (1997). *Integrative Life Planning: Critical Tasks for Career Development and Changing Life Patterns.* San Francisco: Jossey-Bass Inc.

Introduction

Before you begin, it is important to understand what you are going to be doing because it may be a little different from what you have done in the past. This Participant Guide is intended to guide you through an appreciative interview process.

You will be asked questions about times when you saw things working at their best in your work and your life. Many times the focus of the questions in life is on those things that are not working well or the problems you are experiencing, so that you can find the best solution to "fixing" the challenge. This experience is intended to be different: you are asked to try to learn about things at their best — the successes — so that you can find out what works and find ways to infuse more of the positive core into your life and work. This journey encourages both the acceptance of a positive perspective as a world view (in contrast to a deficit-based view), as well as the development of language that supports a more positive process for exploring your career development needs.

The purpose of this process is to create a positive self-image and allow you to envision even greater possibilities based on your strengths. The process will also help you to connect your work and life decisions to others around you who serve life partners and support networks. The end result of the interview will help you better understand the "life-giving" forces that provide vitality and distinctive competence to your life and work.

As a part of this process, you will look at

- The core factors that enable your success
- Your story as it is being written, unfolding in the presence of a dialogue partner through the interview process
- The learning gained from your experience as you examine closely those moments when you have been at your best
- Your most effective practices, strengths, and best qualities that are necessary for you to preserve as you make other changes in your life
- How your positive past — the best of your experiences — can help you be more daring and innovative as you think about your true potential
- The future that you envision for yourself, including your hopes and positive images
- Building a life through positive and intentional planning that integrates the best of who you are with those with whom you share your life

Key Definitions at the Foundation of this Approach

Career is defined as the "totality of work — paid and unpaid — one does in his/her lifetime" (National Career Development Association Web site, http://www.ncda.org/pdf/Policy.pdf).

Career development is "the total constellation of psychological, sociological, educational, physical, economic, and chance factors that combine to influence the nature and significance of work in the total lifespan of any given individual" (National Career Development Association Web site, http://www.ncda.org/pdf/Policy.pdf).

Integrative Life Planning is a comprehensive career development model that brings together many aspects of people's lives in ways that help them to see the "big picture" of their lives, their communities, and the larger society. It is both a philosophical framework and practical strategies that work in harmony with concepts like connectedness, pluralism, spirituality, subjectivity, wholeness and community. It embraces the notion of patterns as fluid, integrative processes that bring parts together to make a whole, as well as the need for reflection on one's developmental priorities for mind, body, and spirit. There are six important principles to Integrative Life Planning: (a) it is a way of seeing the world that takes into account both personal development and the contexts within which we live, (b) it focuses on the value of diversity and inclusivity, (c) it involves the examination of the relationship goals and achievement goals relative to society, the organization, the family, and the individual, (d) it explores connections and links between work and family, (e) it introduces spirituality, meaning, and purpose as key aspects of life planning, and (f) it emphasizes helping people manage change and understand their life choices, decisions, and transitions in a societal context (modified from Hansen, 1997, pp. 11–18).

Life-giving forces are the distinctive strengths that give you life and vitality when you are functioning at your best (modified from Watkins & Mohr, 2001, p. 75). These could include elements or experiences within your past and/or present that represent your strengths when operating at your very best and could be a single moment in time or any aspect that contributes to your highest points and most valued experiences or characteristics (modified from Cooperrider, Whitney & Stavros, 2005, p. 418).

Positive possibilities, also referred to as "provocative propositions," are statements that bridge the best of "what is" with your vision of "what might be." As such, it becomes a written expression of your desired state, written in the present tense, to guide your planning and success in the future (modified from Cooperrider, Whitney & Stavros, 2005, p. 419).

Introduction to the Interview

When you conduct an interview…

The purpose of the interview is about appreciating the interviewee's strengths and exploring what "gives life" and energy to the interviewee. The process is focused on the interviewee initially; you, the interviewer, will get to share your focused listening later in the process.

1. Please read each question or say it in your own words, and then allow time for the interviewee to reflect and answer. Silence is okay, so please do not feel like you need to fill the empty space. If needed, repeat the question if that seems like that might help.

2. Encourage your interviewee to talk. Listen with curiosity and wonder. Nonverbal encouragers like gently nodding your head, taking notes, and demonstrating an active listening posture (facing the interviewee directly, occasionally leaning forward, keeping a comfortable distance between you and the interviewee, and being attentive). Verbal encouragers or prompting such as paraphrasing and asking probing follow-up questions are also useful.

3. Enjoy the experience of learning about someone else and how that person does what she or he does. Smile and remember the more at ease you are, the more at ease the interviewee will be.

4. Make notes as you go and then record key points on the Building on Your Strengths Interview Summary Sheet that follows the interview questions.

5. When the interview is complete, share with your interviewee what you learned that most interested you and thank the person for her or his time.

6. Please be sure to give the interviewee her or his Interview Guide and the Interview Summary Sheet that you completed. This is important since the story the interviewee shared was her or his personal story and she or he is the owner of the product.

Images of My Positive Future

It is time to push the creative edges of possibility and to wonder about your greatest potential, your "calling," and your unique contribution to the world. This is a vital step in the process of creating the images and frameworks that will guide the actions that create your future.

This is also the opportunity to seek out and preserve that which you do best, those characteristics of which you are most proud, and the characteristics that create success and that you wish to build into your future.

Following the guided-imagery activity, please jot down the first few words that capture the images, feelings, and reactions to your experience.

What are you "meant" or "called" to do?

What is the inspiration that supports you?

Locating My Personal Themes

Please take a few moments to consider the themes, patterns, or areas that appeared in the stories and in your dialogue with your partner and in the image of your positive future. Please identify the themes and patterns, and list them here.

What are the root causes of your success? What themes or patterns are at the heart of peak experiences and wishes for the future?

Were any vital life themes or values overlooked in the stories or the guided imagery?

What are the most engaging and exciting possibilities for you as you think about your future life and work?

Creating My Ideal Work-Life Scenario

Capture the engaging and exciting positive possibilities by creating your "Ideal Work-Life Scenario." Let's begin by drawing together the different pieces. Please try to write your statement in the present tense, and be sure it is positive, uses energizing language, and is bold and provocative.

The best work situation for me is one where I . . .

The most important life giving forces that I need to carry forward are . . .

My ideal work-life senario would be . . .

What about ths ideal position gives you energy and a feeling of purpose?

Innovative Ways to Create the Future: My Sequence for Success

Use the following prompts as the basis for your Sequence for Success. Again, please frame your responses in positive, energizing language. For this section, please consider your planning as a continuum from current reality to beyond your expectations.

Please consider your "Ideal Work-life Scenario" as you respond to the following questions.

What could you change, adapt, or adopt in your current situation to get the sense of purpose and energy gained through your ideal position?	If you were to be TEM TIMES MORE BOLD in the pursuit of your ideal work-life scenario, what would you do?

Sequence for Success: Shoulds, Wants, & Will

As you think about your ideal work-life scenario, what are five things from the two previous lists that you feel like you SHOULD be doing to be moving toward the ideal?

1.

2.

3.

4.

5.

WANTS
Benefits/gains/draws on my strength in the area of _____ ?

____.

____.

____.

Action Plan: My "WILL DO" Goal

I will _____

_____

beginning _____ and I will complete this goal by _____.

☐ Yes – able?   ☐ Reflects my ideal?   ☐ Driven by my strengths?   ☐ Within my influence?

I will know I am successful when_____

_____

_____

_____

To Do List: I will accomplish the following steps and tasks to achieve my "will do" goal.
[Please write each task or step to the right of the dash (–).]

(____) – _____

(____) – _____

(____) – _____

(____) – _____

(____) – _____

(____) – _____

(____) – _____

(____) – _____

(____) – _____

(____) – _____

Q1. Is there a sequence that needs to be followed? Use the space between the parentheses to indicate the order.

Q2. What is the smallest step you could take that would have the greatest impact? Mark that step with a star (*).

Action Plan: My "WILL DO" Goal

I will _____

_____

beginning _____ and I will complete this goal by _____.

☐ Yes – able? ☐ Reflects my ideal? ☐ Driven by my strengths? ☐ Within my influence?

I will know I am successful when_____

_____

_____

_____

To Do List: I will accomplish the following steps and tasks to achieve my "will do" goal.
[Please write each task or step to the right of the dash (–).]

(_____) – _____

(_____) – _____

(_____) – _____

(_____) – _____

(_____) – _____

(_____) – _____

(_____) – _____

(_____) – _____

(_____) – _____

(_____) – _____

Q1. Is there a sequence that needs to be followed? Use the spaces to indicate the order.

Q2. What is the smallest step you could take that would have the greatest impact? Mark that step with a star (*).

Cultivating My Sequence for Success

Using the "My Sequence for Success Goals & Action Steps" planning sheet, please review your goals and your action steps using the following steps.

1. *For each of your goals, identify two or three action steps necessary to get that goal moving and heading in the right direction.*

   Consider these four criteria (modified from Cooperrider, Whitney, & Stavros, 2005, p. 140) for thinking through your action steps:

   - Is it a "yes-able" idea (are you likely to get support from the important actors in your life)?
   - Does it address/reflect the underlying principles in your positive possibilities statement?
   - What are you already doing (key success factors) that can be continued or enhanced?
   - What new actions would create an impact?

2. *Identify the goals and action steps that draw on your strengths, life-giving forces, and wishes. Also, identify those goals that will require you to draw on your larger support system?*

   An important component of this plan is identifying which of the items on your list draw on or are driven by your strengths, life-giving forces, or are captured in your wishes for your future. These items likely represent your internal resources and motivators for engaging your plan.

   The goals and action steps for which you draw on others for support are the ones that remain. Do not be afraid to ask for help — consider the other important actors in your life and draw on their strengths. It is important to note that the integration of our lives with the lives of others provides a solid basis of support and a sense that you are part of a community working toward your success.

3. *Identify which of the goals and action steps you are able to do something about and which are within your ability to influence.*

   There are some things we can change, and others that we cannot. Wishing for better weather or hoping that your employer will be fairer are not necessarily within your ability to change. Where you work or the choices you make about how you spend your free time are things you can control and influence. Focusing your time and resources on the positive goals and action steps that are within your control tends to, over time, expand your ability to influence a greater number of outcomes. It might also reduce your frustration over trying to change that which is out of your control.

4. *What is the smallest step (an action, a decision, a behavior) you could take that would have the largest impact?*

   Look over the action steps you have listed and note the ones that draw on your strengths, life-giving forces, and wishes and are also within your area of influence. Which one of those action plan items, if completed, would create the greatest changes? Is there a particular action step or goal that, if accomplished, would result in all the rest falling into place?

Possible Bumps in the Road to Building on My Strengths

It is important to acknowledge and deal with any bumps in the road to building on your strengths, as well as any "areas to manage" of which you are aware.

What are the possible bumps to building on your strengths and achieving your goals and action steps?

Bump	Action
1.	☐ Ignore ☐ Respond ☐ Respond Later
2.	☐ Ignore ☐ Respond ☐ Respond Later
3.	☐ Ignore ☐ Respond ☐ Respond Later
4.	☐ Ignore ☐ Respond ☐ Respond Later

Once the bumps have been identified, use this decision tree:

- Choose the bumps that are within your ability to influence.
- Select your desired action, which could be
  a. Ignoring the bump,
  b. Choosing to deal with the bump later, or
  c. Decide to respond to the bump.
- If you decide to respond, decide who, within the important actors in your life, can assist you in dealing with this bump.
- Be sure to include additional action steps in your Sequence for Success to deal with these bumps.

Sustaining My Positive Possibilities

What is your strategy for sustaining this plan? Sustaining the work you have done depends on your ability to integrate into your perspective the process experienced through this packet. In addition to developing your life-work plan, the goal of this process is to create and enhance your ability to (a) choose a positive focus in your career development inquiries, (b) continuously reflect on your strengths, (c) react to changing circumstances using your "life-giving forces" as a guide, and (d) respond in ways that challenge you and provoke creative responses leading to your successful realization of your future vision for your career and life.

Four competency areas have been identified that may lead to greater progress in productivity, efficiency and performance (modified from Cooperrider, Whitney, & Stavros, 2005, pp. 181–182). Engaging and working through this "Building on Your Strengths" process may enhance your strengths in each of these areas of competence.

Affirmative Competence involves your capacity to appreciate positive possibilities by selectively focusing on current and past strengths, successes, and potentials.

Expansive Competence is your ability to challenge your comfort zone — including but not limited to your habits and conventional practices — by asking yourself how you could be bolder in your efforts, and by prioritizing your efforts not by how easy they are to accomplish but rather by how much the effort contributes to your positive core and life-giving forces. It encourages you to stretch in new directions and encourages you to move toward a more passionate engagement between you and your work, and between you and others who are important actors in your life.

Generative Competence encourages you to strive to understand how the results of your actions contribute to a meaningful purpose for you and society, and to recognize how you understand and experience a sense of progress.

Collaborative Competence is the intentional engagement of the important actors in your life in ongoing dialogue about those things you value most deeply. It also includes how you seek out diverse perspectives to continuously transform your self-image and future possibilities.

Valuing Your Process

Also critical to sustaining your process is finding a way to value what you have completed on a personal level. The final area on the Sequence for Success Goals & Action planning sheet identifies an opportunity for you to consider the impact of this process on your life by asking "This plan responds to my economic, family, spiritual and cultural needs, as well as contributing to important community needs by…"

References & Resources

Buckingham, M., and Clifton, D. O. (2001). *Now, discover your strengths.* New York: The Free Press.

Cooperrider, D. L., Whitney, D., and Stavros, J. M. (2005). *Appreciative Inquiry handbook: The first in a series of AI workbooks for leaders of change.* Brunswick, OH: Crown Custom Publishing, Inc., & San Francisco: Berrett-Koehler Publishers, Inc.

Hammond, S. A. (1996). *The thin book of Appreciative Inquiry* (2nd. Plano, TX: Thin Book Publishing Co.

Hansen, L. S. (1997). *Integrative life planning: Critical tasks for career development and changing life patterns.* San Francisco: Jossey-Bass Inc.

Leider, R. J., and Shapiro, D. A. (1996). *Repacking your bags: Lighten your load for the rest of your life.* San Francisco: Berrett-Koehler Publishers.

Maguire, J. (1998). *The power of personal storytelling: Spinning tales to connect with others.* NY: Jeremy P. Tarcher/Putnam.

Watkins, J. M., and Mohr, B. J. (2001). *Appreciative Inquiry: Change at the speed of imagination.* San Francisco: Jossey-Bass/Pfeiffer.

Valuing the Building on Your Strengths Process

Please respond to the following questions related to how this process worked, what you learned, and how the experience of Building on Your Strengths has influenced you or your work.

What about the Building on Your Strengths approach most enlivened you?

What energizes you about introducing or using this approach in your work or personal life?

What is your "elevator story" about this process that you would like to share?

How could you take this process to a higher level for yourself, someone else, or your organization?

What is one idea or action that you can do tomorrow?

Thank you for your time and participation!

References

Adolescence. (Winter 2004). Review of the book *Authentic happiness: Using the new Positive Psychology to realize your potential for lasting fulfillment. Adolescence,* 39(156), 838-839.

Benson, P. L. (2003). Developmental assets and asset-building community: Conceptual and empirical foundations." In R. M. Lerner & P. L. Benson (Eds.), *Developmental Assets and asset-building communities: Implications for research, policy, and practice.* New York: Kluwer Academic/Plenum Publishers, New York.

Buckingham, M., & Clifton, D. O. (2001). *Now, discover your strengths.* New York: The Free Press.

Buckingham, M., & Coffman, C. (1999). *First, break all the rules: What the world's greatest managers do differently.* New York: Simon & Schuster.

Cook, E.P., Heppner, M. J., & O'Brien (2002). Career development of women of color and white women: Assumptions, conceptualizations and interventions from a Ecological perspective. *The Career Development Quarterly,* 50(4), 291–305.

Cooperrider, D. L., & Whitney, D. (2000). A positive revolution in change: Appreciative Inquiry." In D.L. Cooperrider, P. F. Sorensen, Jr., D. Whitney, & T. F. Yaeger (Eds.), *Appreciative Inquiry: Rethinking human organization toward a positive theory of change.* Champaign, IL: Stipes Publishing L.L.C.

Cooperrider, D. L., & Whitney, D. (2005). *Appreciative Inquiry: A positive revolution in change.* San Francisco: Berrett-Koehler Publishers, Inc.

Cooperrider, D. L., Whitney, D., & Stavros, J. M. (2005). *Appreciative Inquiry handbook: The first in a series of AI workbooks for leaders of change.* Brunswick, OH: Crown Custom Publishing, Inc., & San Francisco: Berrett-Koehler Publishers, Inc.

Hammond, S. A. (1996). *The thin book of Appreciative Inquiry.* Plano, TX: Kodiak Consulting.

Hansen, L. S. (1997). *Integrative life planning: Critical tasks for career development and changing life patterns.* San Francisco: Jossey-Bass Publishers, Inc.

Peterson, C., & Seligman, M. E. P (2004) *Character strengths and virtues: A handbook and classification.* New York: American Psychological Association and Oxford University Press, Inc

Preskill, H., & Coghlan, A. T. (Eds). (Winter 2003). *New directions for evaluation, No. 100: Using Appreciative Inquiry in evaluation.* San Francisco: Wiley Periodicals, Inc.

Search Institute. (2007). *Making a difference for young people: The power of one.* Retrieved March 27, 2007, from http://www.searchinstitute.org/assets/individual/ThePowerOfOne.html

Seligman, M. E. P. (2002). *Authentic happiness: Using the new Positive Psychology to realize your potential for lasting fulfillment.* New York: The Free Press.

Seligman, M. E. P., Steen, T. A., Park, N., & Peterson, C. (July-August 2005). Positive Psychology progress: Empirical validation of interventions. *American Psychologist,* 60 (5), 410-421.

Super, D. E., Savickas, M. L., & Super, C. M. (1996). The Life-Span, Life-Space approach to careers. In D. Brown, L. Brooks, and associates, *Career choice and development.* San Francisco: Jossey-Bass Inc., Publishers.

Watkins, J. M., & Mohr, B. J. (2001). *Appreciative Inquiry: Change at the speed of imagination.* San Francisco: Jossey-Bass/Pfeiffer.

Whitney, D., Cooperrider, D., Trosten-Bloom, A., & Kaplin, B. S. (2002). *Encyclopedia of positive questions: Volume one: Using Appreciative Inquiry to bring out the best in your organization.* Euclid, OH: Lakeshore Communications.